The
Christ of Lent

by

Olin S. Reigstad

Published by Augsburg Publishing House · Minneapolis

THE CHRIST OF LENT
Copyright 1944
Augsburg Publishing House

Printed in the United States of America by
Augsburg Publishing House, Minneapolis 15, Minnesota

Contents

44291

Chapter 1

Jesus Faces a Crisis

Then was Jesus led up of the spirit into the wilderness to be tempted of the devil.

And when he had fasted forty days and forty nights, he was afterward an hungred.

And when the tempter came to him, he said, If thou be the Son of God, command that these stones be made bread.

But he answered and said, It is written, Man shall not live by bread alone, but by every word that proceedeth out of the mouth of God.

Then the devil taketh him up into the holy city, and setteth him on a pinnacle of the temple,

And saith unto him, If thou be the Son of God, cast thyself down: for it is written, He shall give his angels charge concerning thee: and in their hands they shall bear thee up, lest at any time thou dash thy foot against a stone.

Jesus said unto him, It is written again, Thou shalt not tempt the Lord thy God.

Again, the devil taketh him up into an exceeding high mountain, and sheweth him all the kingdoms of the world, and the glory of them;

And saith unto him, All these things will I give thee, if thou wilt fall down and worship me.

Then saith Jesus unto him, Get thee hence, Satan: for it is written, Thou shalt worship the Lord thy God, and him only shalt thou serve.

Then the devil leaveth him, and, behold, angels came and ministered unto him.

Matthew 4:1-11

WE believe that Jesus was without sin. That axiomatic statement is scriptural and must be regarded as one of the cornerstones of the Christian faith. A single transgression either by commission or omission would have unfitted Him for the part He assumed in God's economy of salvation. A guilty thought or word or deed proceeding from Him would have caused the whole "plan of grace to miscarry." He needed to be spotless as our sacrifice and He was approved by the strictest law of righteousness. Even atheism and infidelity have eloquently praised His unsullied purity and goodness. Men are strangely unanimous in admitting His goodness.

The righteousness of Jesus cost Him a great deal, and He was not sinless from necessity. His purity had to be maintained in untold stubborn conflicts. The trials of moral warfare He knew well. He assumed the risks, the necessities of a human life—He took with human nature all its infirmities, hazards, and sorrows and thus became subject to its tears and pains and became liable to temptation and sin and discomfiture. He was called upon to face the exposure and the hazard of all evil common to human life. "It behooved him in all things to be like unto his brethren." "He was made under the law" and "compassed with infirmity" and "in all points tempted like as we are." So the Word of God teaches and we have no other guide. As a result of vigilance and heroic faithfulness He won for us and for all men of all time a moral victory. It might have been otherwise.

This temptation in the wilderness was not the only conflict Jesus knew. His whole life was one of conflict—a conflict with sin and wrong. This temptation stands at the very beginning of His ministry and was very deep and sore. The peril and assault of Satan's effort to mislead the Savior, brought all His moral strength to the test and pained the depths of His mysterious nature.

There were two agencies concerned in the temptation. The first was God Himself, for Jesus "was led up of the Spirit." It represented God's plan —and He plans well. As the sufferings and death of Jesus were divinely planned, so it was also divinely appointed that He must meet Satan and withstand whatever assaults his malignant subtilty might invent. It represents the first stage of His amazing suffering for the world. The form of the

temptation was a product of the second agency—
the devil.

There are well-meaning people who doubt the
existence of the devil, and he himself has always
sought to persuade men that there is no such evil
creature. Revelation on that subject, however, is
very clear. From the very beginning the sacred
writers have never lost sight of that great malignant spiritual power, the adversary of God and
all that which is good,—whose baneful influence
has tracked the human family from Paradise to
our modern everyday experiences. Rationalism has
insisted that God would be too good to allow the
existence of a power so vast and ruinous. But it
is a matter of common experience that evil men
are permitted to live in spite of their wickedness.
If it is inconsistent with divine excellence to permit evil to exist in one case, it is equally so in another.

The exact form or method Satan employed
when he made these subtle and fruitless stabs at
the Son of God is not revealed. Martin Luther believed that Satan appeared as an angel of light.
Others maintain that it was a vision. The truth is
we do not know. Nor is it necessary that we should
know. The temptation was real and searching.

The temptation came to Jesus immediately after the miraculous and exalting experience associated with His baptism by John the Baptist at

the River Jordan, when the heavens were opened
and He was acclaimed the Son of God. It was an
extraordinary experience and in its afterglow Satan accosted Him. Satan often attacks when the
heart is joyful, and when the spirit has been quick-
ened his assaults are fierce and deadly. We would
say that his attacks are strategic—he is familiar
with spots that are vulnerable. He expects the
light and happiness of the occasion to hide his approach.

When God's servants are ready for duty, the
devil cannot rest and the storms begin to blow.
Half-hearted Christians, who compromise truth
and principle, the devil does not fear. But the
Christ and the Christ-like he cannot abide. These
arouse his malignity and he comes upon them in
the most unexpected moments. He seeks to shake
their faith and courage at the very beginning or
he deceives them into believing in an easy victory.
Maybe he crowds the path with adversity—but be
sure, he always strikes in the most tender places.

Jesus was tempted in the wilderness. Unten-
anted and undisturbed were the environs of His
habitation. A season of solitude and an uninter-
rupted communion with God the Father was emi-
nently needful. God has prepared great spiritual
leaders in the same way. Moses needed years alone
in the Arabian wilderness to be perfected for his
task. John the Baptist was hidden in seclusion un-

til he appeared as a voice in the wilderness. Saul of Tarsus went into Arabia to adjust himself to his great work and to commune with his God. Luther was fashioned for his task in a monastery cell and in the seclusion of a niche in the Wartburg.

Great souls are often starved for the want of seclusion, a place of quietude. Too much pressing business, too many cares, too many friends. So much occupied that they have little time remaining to learn a little of themselves, their God, and their Bible. More of the retirement and the wilderness experiences are needed by most of us.

From the experiences of Jesus it is evident that solitude has its dangers. To be excluded from the din of the world does not necessarily mean that we are safe. The devil is in the wilderness as well as upon the crowded highways and thoroughfares of life. In the common world much of his work is done by agents,—in solitude he attacks directly. The most horrible crimes are those clothed in secrecy. There imaginations are polluted, souls are debauched, lives are lost. Like an unfailing rock, Noah stood in the midst of a world flooded with sin and apostasy, but he fell when the world was gone and he was alone in his tent. The vileness of Sodom and Gomorrah did not destroy Lot, but in the lonely mountains of Zoar he was corrupted by his own lusts. And nowhere did the blessed Savior encounter so much infernal treach-

ery as in the wilderness when He was alone. For
Him it was a place of victory. There He was led
by the Spirit and there His first victory was won.
The greatest victory and the greatest achievement
are won usually in solitude.

When the temptation of Jesus was finished "the
angels came and ministered to him." The angels
were laden with comfort and abundant consolation. The first great crisis had been met and Jesus was the master then as now. Jesus leaned on
the Word of God and learned in His trial the les-
sons of self-denial, patience, and fidelity.

Let us learn from Jesus to trust the Word of
God and say with Him, "It is written." Then shall
we too share in the gracious ministration of angels.

Chapter 2

A Faithless
Generation Befriended

And one of the multitude answered and said, Master, I have brought unto thee my son, which hath a dumb spirit;

And wheresoever he taketh him, he teareth him: and he foameth, and gnasheth with his teeth, and pineth away: and I spake to thy disciples that they should cast him out; and they could not.

He answereth him, and saith, O faithless generation, how long shall I be with you? how long shall I suffer you? bring him unto me.

And they brought him unto him: and when he saw him, straightway the spirit tare him; and he fell on the ground, and wallowed foaming.

And he asked his father, How long is it ago since this came unto him? And he said, Of a child.

And ofttimes it hath cast him into the fire, and into the waters, to destroy him: but if thou canst do any thing, have compassion on us, and help us.

Jesus said unto him, If thou canst believe, all things are possible to him that believeth.

And straightway the father of the child cried out, and said with tears, Lord, I believe; help thou mine unbelief.

When Jesus saw that the people came running together, he rebuked the foul spirit, saying unto him, Thou dumb and deaf spirit, I charge thee, come out of him, and enter no more into him.

And the spirit cried, and rent him sore, and came out of him: and he was as one dead; insomuch that many said, He is dead.

But Jesus took him by the hand, and lifted him up; and he arose.

And when he was come into the house, his disciples asked him privately, Why could not we cast him out?

And he said unto them, This kind can come forth by nothing, but by prayer and fasting.

Mark 9:17-29

WE had thought—maybe as the children grow older things will be better. There seemed to be so many things to worry about when they were small. But they grew older and our anxieties only multiplied. We have concluded that whether they are children nestled in the crib or they are stationed at some army camp or facing death upon the battlefront, the parents will have enough to bear—too much, in fact, without the grace of God. There is no anxiety more real than the mental and spiritual distress that parents endure for their children. The wakeful nights—the long, lonely vigils at the sick bed—when we cry, "Watchman, what of the night," will morning never come?

Never did we know that the pain of another could become so real, until we shared the suffering of our children. And when God, in spite of our care and nurture plucked the little flower from our hands, it was as if something were taken out of us.

Down in southern Wisconsin sixty years ago, a young husband and wife builded a cabin in a little clearing. Forest blackness surrounded them on every hand, but there in this little quiet space they builded their home, and a little boy came to bless the happy union. Sunshine girded the little clearing and the voice of happy laughter could be heard. Almost two years of happiness had they enjoyed when that strange visitor came. What a terrible thing when doctors are few and far away when illness comes. For days the little life hung in the balance, and father and mother alternated at the bedside and then on his very birthday, the angels came and took the child. It was a hard experience, and that mother never after was quite the same. No, she didn't become hard or bitter, or indifferent—it didn't take away happiness, but it filled the heart with a strange yearning. After that she seemed to be half here and half in heaven. Now we might have said to her, "It is better so," but to bear the affliction and remain the same is quite a different matter.

One thing is certain. There are many things worse than death. The father in our text today was enduring a bitterness worse than death. What a terrible affliction had come upon that family. It does not say how old the son was, it only says he had been afflicted since childhood. They had done everything possible for the child but to no avail. At last, in desperation and with a frantic hope the father brings him to the disciples; but they were helpless. Their success had made them perfunctory, and matters of such serious import could not be handled in that way. Just then Jesus returns from the mount where He has been transfigured, and He sees the multitude gathered. Jesus asks why so many have gathered and the distracted father of the lad tells his sad story. We say again, many things could be worse than death.

We have seen the feeble-minded and our hearts have bled for the parents. How often the parents have said of such a one, "If God would only take him home." And I believe God must have planned great things in heaven for those who have had so little here. Since God lets them live, that must be best. He understands—we do not. Parents have stood over a child who has been maimed for life and they have said, "Death were better."

Worse still does the affliction become when the child is wayward and serves sin. And if the parental pain and anxiety are real when they stand at the sick bed, how real does the pain become when the child adds transgression upon transgression

and sinks deeper and deeper into the quagmire of
sin. God pity the child who becomes the bitterness
of her who bare him. He were better dead.

And yet whatever the affliction may be, what a
boon that flame of hope is. Parental hope is hard
to kill. This distracted father had been disappointed often, but there was still hope. Wherever love
is, hope lingers. Years of sorrow and disappointment may destroy the element of expectation but
the yearning is still there. Whatever the expectation, this father was sure of what he wanted for
the boy and himself and he made a final heart-
breaking appeal to Jesus saying, "If thou canst do
anything, have compassion on us and help us." I
have no silver, I am not a man of standing, I have
no name, but, "Lord, I believe, help thou mine
unbelief."

And the Lord's help was forthcoming and immediate. How fortunate that he brought his child
to Jesus. He never failed anyone who called upon
His name. "He is the same, yesterday, today and
forever."

How strange that many seek the help of the
church only as a last resort. They do not need the
church until affliction comes. Should we say to
them, "You take care of yourself, you are not one
of us"? Should we scold and say, "Why didn't you
come to us before?" We should do as Jesus did. He
made no reference to past neglect. It is not for us

to catechize, it is for us to help. Where men dazed by sorrow or crazed by sin seek Christian help, we praise God for it, though it may be a belated coming.

There are many difficulties the Christian may be called upon to solve that seem easy. The disciples of Jesus had been successful before, it had been easy for them. But now they were in trouble. The affliction was worse than they anticipated. Jesus told them it must be treated with much fasting and prayer. There are many evils which the church may help to correct, but it will require incessant prayer and sacrifice.

We feel often how little faith we have when we are called upon to deal with real problems, both temporal and spiritual. Has it ever been otherwise? To whom did Jesus say, "O ye of little faith," or whom did He call "a faithless generation"? Did He say that to the scribes or to the thoughtless? No, he said it to those who were near to Him, for "his nearest of kin did not believe on him." We are told that "his disciples believed as yet not the Scriptures," and that the two on the way to Emmaus were "slow to believe." When the scoffer sees how little the Christian can accomplish he says, "Where is your God?" Maybe sometimes we say weeping, "Oh, that I knew where I could find him." Even from the Machaerus prison cell which held the captive eagle, John the Baptist, comes the refrain of doubt, "Art thou he that cometh?" How tremulous the hand of faith is even in the strong—how much has been lost from the cup of blessing. We must pray as did the disciples —"Lord, add to our faith," or as the distracted father did, "Lord, I believe, help thou mine unbelief."

But Jesus deals kindly with men in spite of their infirmities. Did He not commend the faith of the woman from Canaan? We need to say often, "Not all things are clear to me, but help me anyway and then build up my faith." He understands weak faith and He told His disciples to "tarry one for another." We have been enjoined to "receive him that is weak in faith." It is so in the way of faith also that one can make more rapid progress than another. Let us be careful not to despise those who may seem to be weak. In school some pupils learn rapidly, others may be slow. Maybe the teacher sometimes gets impatient with the one who retards the class. But whether it is pedagogically correct or incorrect, many a slow scholar has caught up with the class because a patient teacher tarried for him.

Jesus has not only the love that is willing, but the power that is able to build our faith and grant us far and exceeding more than we ask. Has He ever touched you—or have you as much as touched the hem of His garment?—then you will know.

Chapter 3

The Devil Goes to Church

And in the synagogue there was a man, which had a spirit of an unclean devil, and cried out with a loud voice,
Saying, Let us alone; what have we to do with thee, thou Jesus of Nazareth? art thou come to destroy us? I know thee who thou art; the Holy One of God.
And Jesus rebuked him, saying, Hold thy peace, and come out of him. And when the devil had thrown him in the midst, he came out of him, and hurt him not.
And they were all amazed, and spake among themselves, saying, What a word is this! for with authority and power he commandeth the unclean spirits, and they come out.
And the fame of him went out into every place of the country round about.   Luke 4:33-37

THE devil goes to church and learns something. There were good people and there were bad people in the synagogue that day and the devil was in the midst of them. They all listened and so did he, for Jesus the Holy One of God spoke. The

ministry of Jesus falls into a period when terrible
conditions prevailed and the need of His time was
unspeakable.

We are struck with the fact that Jesus, during
our Lenten season texts, is repeatedly encounter-
ing the evil spirits. The forces of evil seem to be
maneuvering for a place that shall be advantageous
when the final conflict comes between light and
darkness.

Following His usual custom, Jesus comes to the
synagogue on the Sabbath day and avails Himself
of the common privilege, not only to hear but also
to participate in the spiritual discussion and to
elaborate further upon the Scriptures before
them. His participation seems to have had now as
always a telling effect upon the worshippers that
day. His speaking was so dead in earnest—He was
dynamic, magnetic, and the words that He spoke
were vibrant with life and vitality. There was a
marked difference between His preaching and
the cold, frigid interpretations to which they had
become accustomed. Men felt their hearts gripped;
they were touched. There was such a note of sym-
pathy and understanding, a lowly humility that
won not only their admiration but their confidence
as well. For the forces of evil, things didn't look
any too good. How enraged the scribes and Pharisees must have been, sensing that He touched the
hearts of the people deeply. Likely whisperings

went among them, that this man must not be tolerated. His popularity with a nitwit people endangered their very bread and butter income— He was making a bid for recognition that later on might be hard to check. For didn't the people say, "He spoke with authority and not as the scribes." His presentation of the word of God was a reflection upon these men who occupied the ancient offices and were clothed by tradition in high dignity.

How did the people come to be drawn so closely to Jesus? They were quick to recognize that His life was holy and pure. He didn't destroy by His life what He sought to build up by His preaching. His life was unblamable, pure as crystal, white as snow. The people were drawn to Him because of His exemplary walk. Not so with the proud, arrogant scribes who prayed on the street corners to be seen of men. They despoiled widows' properties— they were envious, misinterpreting the word of God. They drew their garments aside lest they should touch the sinner. Their lives ruined whatever vital truths their preaching contained.

So today, one element which the preacher of God's Word must possess, is the power to overcome —to master sin, lest people should say with Paul, "Thou who wouldst teach others, teachest thou not thyself?" How much more the ministry of today could accomplish—how much more power the message might hold if our lives were purer. A purified ministry means a powerful ministry.

Jesus could speak with authority too, because He was the Son of God. Surely He by whom all things were created, must have authority and His message would be conveyed with power.

The message of today as in the time of the scribes may not lose all power when it is delivered by an unbeliever, but I am persuaded much of the power is gone. The better part of it is gone. The persuasive testimony of one who really believes will reach far.

Then too, Jesus was set to accomplish one task and all His power was concentrated upon that work. The scribes frittered away their energies with disputes and arguments and fine distinctions until they forgot the purpose of their ministry. Is there not a danger that the pulpit today may lose its power because the pastor is required to dabble with too many tasks which divide his interest and energy and take away the power which concentration upon one task would create? He is prepared to do one thing, and commanded to do just that one thing—"to preach the Gospel in season and out of season." It is enough if he can talk intelligently and scripturally about sin and grace—and if his life is commendable, as any minister's ought to be, he can do that with authority and power. He can add to his testimony, "Thus saith the

Lord." That's final, conclusive, and beyond any argument by people who accept the Word of God as inspired and infallible.

Now Jesus that day in the synagogue was offensive to the devil. In fact, that evil spirit was very rudely treated. If Satan had planned a coup that day he was sorely disappointed for he was shamefully defeated, disgraced, and driven out.

The church is the representative today through which the Son of God speaks. Would you expect the attitude of the devil to be any different than when he was angered at Jesus? If the church lifts her voice against the social evils, then the world says we are interfering. Leave us alone and we will leave you alone—so the world suggests. A little spirit of compromise they say. Let the church lift her voice against drunkenness and the vile, lawless, incorrigible liquor interests, and at once we are charged with being a lot of old, narrow fogies who are seeking to take man's liberty away from him. If the church lifts her voice against corruption in the community—and God knows that there is enough in any city right now to keep an honest grand jury busy till judgment come—then the church is mixing interests—getting into politics. Have we lost our citizenship because we are Christians? Moses, Jeremiah, Paul, and Luther were not afraid that they were mixing the functions of church and state. If the church lifts her voice against the moral looseness of flaming youth —and what is worse yet, flaming manhood and womanhood—then such subjects have no place in the pulpit. The devil would have us deal so tenderly and delicately with sin that no one would know just what we meant. It's the old, old story— "Thou art come to destroy us." Yes, and when the church ceases to expose sin and in the name of the Son of God to destroy sin, her function is over. Such a church is useless and impotent.

Leading magazines are filled with articles about the church and her dwindling power. Why? Certainly not because she has been old-fashioned enough to proclaim the unadulterated Word of God as revealed in the Holy Scriptures—but because modernism is the creator of compromise. "Eternal vigilance is the price of liberty" in the church too.

When evil is routed and Satan is defeated, be sure he will turn to do you as much harm as he can. The forces of evil will employ every opportunity to destroy the church. But I remember that Jesus once said, "The gates of hell shall not prevail against it." For that assurance we are grateful.

> Oh, do not pray for easy lives;
> Pray to be stronger men.
> Do not pray for tasks equal to your powers;
> Pray for powers equal to your tasks.
>
> PHILLIPS BROOKS

Chapter 4

Stumbling at the Truth

The Jews therefore strove among themselves, saying, How can this man give us his flesh to eat?

Then Jesus said unto them, Verily, verily, I say unto you, Except ye eat the flesh of the Son of man, and drink his blood, ye have no life in you.

Whoso eateth my flesh, and drinketh my blood, hath eternal life; and I will raise him up at the last day.

For my flesh is meat indeed, and my blood is drink indeed.

He that eateth my flesh, and drinketh my blood, dwelleth in me, and I in him.

As the living Father hath sent me, and I live by the Father: so he that eateth me, even he shall live by me.

This is that bread which came down from heaven: not as your fathers did eat manna, and are dead: he that eateth of this bread shall live for ever.

These things said he in the synagogue, as he taught in Capernaum.

Many therefore of his disciples, when they had heard this, said, This is an hard saying; who can hear it?

When Jesus knew in himself that his disciples murmured at it, he said unto them, Doth this offend you?

What and if ye shall see the Son of man ascend up where he was before?

It is the spirit that quickeneth; the flesh profiteth nothing: the words that I speak unto you, they are spirit, and they are life.

But there are some of you that believe not. For Jesus knew from the beginning who they were that believed not, and who should betray him.

And he said, Therefore said I unto you, that no man can come unto me, except it were given unto him of my Father.   John 6:52-65

IT was pathetically tragic to see the thinning ranks as the popularity of Jesus waned. "From that time on, many of his disciples walked no more with him." Why did many of the followers desert Him? Because what He told them was a hard saying. His doctrine and speech had become offensive. What He taught was contrary to their prejudices and to them very absurd, not to say unreasonable. It was not the first time that He encountered that attitude, in fact, He often seemed absurd. His teaching today approaches the climax of absurdity. "Whoso eateth my flesh and drinketh my blood hath eternal life, and I will raise him up at the last day." Whether they understood Him or not, the fact is that from then on a large number of His disciples left Him.

The truth often is distasteful and incomprehensible to the natural man. But that does not alter the fact of truth. The truth is and remains the same whatever our attitude may be. North is north and south is south, whether I believe it or not. The truth imbedded in the law of gravitation may be offensive, and the truth of an algebraic equation may work against us, and yet these truths remain the same. They are as unchangeable as God from whom they proceed.

Why Jesus should necessarily have used the particular terminology He employed that day while addressing the people, we perhaps will never understand. The language was offensive to the great majority of those who heard Him, but it did poignantly illustrate what He so earnestly sought to impress upon them. How patient He had been with the people who followed Him we can never know—and yet in spite of His patient forbearance they persisted in misunderstanding His plan and His mission. They missed the purpose of His entire ministry. He was not come to restore the glory of an old monarchy—He was not come to establish a kingdom of this world—He was not come to vanquish the nations and to raise Judah to political preeminence. And with one master stroke of wisdom He sets forth the real purpose of His advent, and as might have been expected, cleared the atmosphere of doubt and misunderstanding and separated His followers into two groups, those who continued to follow Him and those who refused to continue. There was now no ambiguity and no further need of straddling the issues. You are either for me or against me. The division was effectively accomplished by what He said. The large group of disciples was purged of those who would use Jesus only as an expedient. Those who understood His word properly and in spite of the strange and high claims registered there, chose to continue with Him, were indeed the faithful few who clung to Him until the very last. He became their all in all. They found happiness in their union with Him.

But Jesus has always been offensive in the doctrines He taught. He was a stumbling block to the Jews and an offence to the cultured Greeks and Romans. Men are offended today for precisely the same reason as the Jews and Greeks. Men are still saying that the teaching of Jesus was absurd, or they seek by some means, fair or foul, to so utterly change the meaning of what He said. The "blood theology" is purposely irritating, for that is the only way the crowd can be separated and the children of God stand out in bold relief. If it were not for the apparent absurdities, the world would shield itself within the church—take refuge there to hide their sins and follies. And where the church harbors the world, the truth has not been spoken frankly and without equivocation. The world does not feel at home, nor the sinful at ease where they must constantly face the truth. Then men will either say, "I believe, Lord," or "This is an hard saying, who can hear it?" If that division were needless God would not have insisted upon it. Drag the world with its hypocrisy, its sin and rottenness into the church, tolerate flagrant denials, and you drive the truth out. God has indeed been tolerant to endure congregations and pastors who have deliberately denied the name of the Son of God. But let the world do its worst—the life and integrity of the church may be impaired and imperiled, but never destroyed; and a day of judgment is coming.

Now what is our attitude to the words of Jesus? That is the important question for all of us. Let us look at the claims of Jesus for a moment.

Every living thing must eat to be nourished. That biological law no man would contradict. That law holds good in respect of all life whether it be the simple primary cell or the highest form of life known. But the foods vary. Now the Christian has two lives to be nourished—the physical and the spiritual. The body requires food and most people observe certain rules in feeding that body to promote health and efficiency. The subject of food is a great subject and a profitable one I think—in spite of the fact that the generation which just passed knew neither calories nor vitamines. But all must eat. Our bodies, taken from the earth and returning to the earth again, shall be sustained by the earth. The earning of money with which to buy food, and the preparation of food occupy a great deal of our time. We take our last dime and spend it for food—mortgage our home if need be and cash in on insurance policies to make that possible.

We are never too busy to eat. We sometimes say we are, but really never. Sometimes sickness comes and the desire to eat is gone and the physician prescribes some tonic to increase our desire for food—for only the dead do not eat. "In the Egyptian excavations bodies have been found buried with rations of corn and wheat, but after several thousand years when those sepulchres revealed their secrets, the corn and the wheat were still there, for the dead do not eat."

Now what kind of food must the Christian eat in order that his spiritual life may be preserved? For there is life and that life must be nourished. Jesus answers that question for us: "I am the living bread which came down from heaven: if any man eat of this bread, he shall live forever." This is what caused the protest from the Jews. They didn't question the spiritual life. They admitted its presence, but questions involved the manner of feeding. When Jesus senses that His language has offended them doesn't He moderate His reply to their objection? Emphatically, No! He only reiterates what He has already said in a language that is more emphatic and more offensive. "Verily, I say unto you, Except ye eat the flesh of the Son of man and drink his blood, ye have no life in you."

Jesus is the food of the Christian. That much is clear. Jesus must be accepted by faith. To eat is to receive, to believe in Him is to trust in Him. But He must be received in His entirety, we must accept a full and complete Christ. Only an entire Christ contains all the food elements and all the vitamines sufficient to create and maintain a vigorous, healthy spiritual life. Of course, the language Christ used was figurative and descriptive but very effective. Christ must be absorbed—all that He is and all that He has done for us must really become ours.

Now what have some done in seeking to satisfy their hunger? They trust in Christ as a great leader—and He was that, but He was much more. I must be nourished by more than that because I am not able to follow Him. To trust in Him as a leader only means spiritual malnutrition. Some accept Him as a great preacher—and He was that. "Never man spake as this man." But that truth, great as it is, will never satisfy a sinful, hungry world. The more beautiful, forceful and effective His sermons are, the more intensely will a soul hunger after life. Sermons only quicken the spiritual appetite—they are stimulants, tonics, but if that is all, He leaves us miserable and impotent. Others have followed Him as a great example—and He was that. A perfect example to follow but still we are helpless. I want to be like Him but I cannot be. His example makes me more miserably hungry. We have referred to three elements in Christ and there is strength in all of them when properly absorbed—but there is infinitely more. We must accept Him in His fulness, in His entirety. Strange how many will accept Him as a leader, a teacher, or preacher, or as an example, and yet refuse to accept Him as the Savior and atoner. They lacerate Christ. And no man can subsist spiritually on a dismembered Christ. Accept Christ in that way and the hunger pains only increase. It's like drinking salt water to satisfy your thirst.

Do you believe that He made full atonement for all your sins and for the sins of the world? Our attitude toward Him will not change the effectiveness of His life and death. He is in all His person, in all His lowliness and in all His majesty the only food that will nourish a sin-sick world back to life and health.

He died for me, and without that death, without that shedding of blood there could have been no atonement, and without that I cannot be one with God, and hence not saved. Only when we accept Him, trust in Him, rest in Him, consume Him as our great Redeemer have we assimilated the food which is needful for our souls. How God could provide salvation in that way may be a mystery. So there is something mysterious about the food which daily nourishes our physical life. We don't stop to investigate. We eat because we are nourished. Stop investigating Christ and receive Him as He comes to you in the Word of God and you will have the happy experience of learning by observation that He satisfies.

Thanks be to God for everything.

Chapter 5

The Magnificat

MARY'S SONG OF PRAISE

And Mary said, My soul doth magnify the Lord,
And my spirit hath rejoiced in God my Saviour.
For he hath regarded the low estate of his hand-
maiden: for, behold, from henceforth all generations
shall call me blessed.
For he that is mighty hath done to me great things;
and holy is his name.
And his mercy is on them that fear him from genera-
tion to generation.
He hath shewed strength with his arm; he hath scat-
tered the proud in the imagination of their hearts.
He hath put down the mighty from their seats, and
exalted them of low degree.
He hath filled the hungry with good things; and the
rich he hath sent empty away.
He hath holpen his servant Israel, in remembrance of
his mercy;
As he spake to our fathers, to Abraham, and to his
seed for ever.

Luke 1:46-55

THE Lenten season is essentially one of deep and earnest introspection. The colors are sombre, for here we have the conflict between good and evil pressed to its extremity. Dark clouds hang ominously upon the world and its benighted people. We are facing an inevitable conflict unto death. The sins of the world, yours and mine, are about to be atoned. And in the process of the conflict the morning stars will cease their singing and nature will struggle in despair while the Son of man is lifted up before the world on "Skull Hill." But another day will dawn when, after the turmoil of crucifixion, the serpent shall writhe in the dust in wounded agony, while the Son of man, dying, still lives. The shades of night shall flee and the sunshine of Easter day shall flood every nook and corner of Calvary's Hill until men shall see its glory and be glad. The voice of weeping shall become a song of joyous praise. "Great things hath the Lord done for us, whereof we are glad."

We have a song before us today—Mary's song of praise, Mary the mother of Jesus. Her heart is filled with a pious, ravishing joy. The song she sings is an expression of joy. The words are poured forth from a heart filled with love, and to reveal fully the indescribable thoughts and ecstasies which overwhelm her, she resorts to words of Scripture so close to her heart. "My soul doth magnify the Lord, and my spirit hath rejoiced in

God my Savior." "From henceforth all generations shall call me blessed." Her name is not forgotten, and so long as Jesus is proclaimed it shall be remembered. Her memory will be precious and holy so long as the Scriptures are read, and the Christian church repeats its creed, "I believe in Jesus Christ, His only begotten Son, conceived by the Holy Ghost, and born of the Virgin Mary." She shall always bear womanhood's greatest distinction and be called "the mother of our Lord." But we do not believe that Mary was born without sin, nor that she continued sin-free and innocent. We do not worship her, for we believe that there is only one God and one mediator between God and man, that man Christ Jesus. We do not ask her intercession before the throne of grace for one makes intercession for us and that is Christ. We have one advocate with the Father, and that is Jesus Christ the righteous. That however does not prevent us from giving Mary a choice place in the history of God's Kingdom. She is the glorious product of the old covenant, and yet the soul in which the new has found its richest and noblest expression. She stands forth as a beautiful example for generations to emulate.

Moses in the wilderness for lack of faith pleaded to be excused from the task assigned to him, and yet in the Old Testament he was perhaps the greatest of the great. Jonah, sent to Nineveh, flees from his task until God recalls him from his error. Sara in the doorway of her tent laughs in doubt as the angel proclaims that a son shall be born to her in her advanced years. Zacharias in the temple demanded a sign so that he might be sure of the Lord's word. But when the angel came to Mary, she said, "Be it unto me according to thy word." And Elizabeth her kinswoman poured forth her heart with joy saying, "Blessed is she that believed, for there shall be a performance of those things promised by the Lord."

It was a faith-testing proclamation that came to Mary. What would her people say? What would Joseph, her betrothed, say? Obstacles and hindrances there were—plenty of them, to have caused her to turn away from the heavenly messenger. But she replied, "Behold, the handmaid of the Lord." I am ready. Something so tender and delicate about her willing personality which finds here a beautiful acquiescence.

Clothed in deep humility she is the servant and "handmaid of the Lord." She may be worshipped by some but she thinks of God as her Savior. Spirit-filled she bursts forth into the poetic strains of the Magnificat. She praises, extols, magnifies the power and might, the holiness and mercy of God. She stands at the apex of a vast company of people and she receives the fulfillment of God's long-expected promise. From Paradise to Nazareth

was about four thousand years. Generations had
come and gone but the cherubic promise from the
tragic drama of Paradise had not been forgotten.
The voices of Abraham, Isaac and Jacob which res-
onantly reiterated the promise received by them
had long been hushed, but the words they had
uttered had become a rich treasure for the Hebrew
people. The prophet voices of Judah that had
spoken so clearly about the Messiah had been
silent about four hundred years and the parch-
ments that bore their words were greying with age.
But at last—when the earth is covered with darkness, the voice of God is heard once more in Nazareth. Mary of the lineage of David is to be the
mother of the Messiah. All the prophecies have
merged and tapered until they fall upon the peasant woman in Galilee. The time is close at hand.
No wonder there is an outburst of song. To have
such an intimate part in the fulfillment of ancient
prophecy and such an honored part in God's eternal plan must be grounds sufficient for an everlasting song. But Mary's joy was not selfish for she
elaborates upon God's mighty achievements for all
the people and she dwells upon and magnifies His
divine attributes.

Now there may be many kinds of joy but none
can endure save true joy which is spiritual and
eternal. There are things that feign to bring joy
but how soon are they lost. Happiness that is de-

pendent upon material things doesn't last long. The joys connected with perishable things evanesce, disappear—leaving only a sorrowful, vacuous memory. Not so with joy that has its origin in the Lord. No power in earth can take that away. That is why the Christian more than anyone else should live a joyous and happy life. The Holy Scriptures ring from beginning to end with a joyous refrain for the people of God. "Serve the Lord with gladness, come before his presence with singing;" "The voice of rejoicing and salvation is in the tabernacles of the righteous"; "Therefore with joy shall ye draw water out of the wells of salvation." And in the New Testament the kingdom is called "righteousness, peace, and joy in the Holy Ghost." "The fruit of the Spirit is love, joy, and peace." "Rejoice that your names are written in heaven." "Pray and ye shall receive, that your joy may be full." And Paul says finally, "Rejoice in the Lord always, again I say rejoice."

There is abundant evidence that the Christian state should be a happy and joyous one. An utter lack of joy should make us question the reality of our faith. The anemic joy and the dyspeptic countenance are not marks of superiority. The contrary is true. According to Paul, the Christian is always "sorrowful yet always rejoicing."

When there are so many who have little or no joy, must we not ask what the real cause may be?

I believe the question can be answered. Our religion has not become personal enough. It has not been vitalized. Our personal experience is not adequate. Maybe we have been resting too much upon what others have accomplished for us. Maybe we have not come through with a definite conviction of sin and grace. If a real consciousness of sin overtakes us, if our lives are turned inside out until all we have done is bared before the flaming eye of a perfect God, and then under the fear and apprehension of a summary judgment, hear God by His grace saying, "Fear not," do not be afraid, "Go and sin no more." "For evil I will give good, for death I will give life." O, what unspeakable joy to know that God cares and forgives. Take down the harp and sing, lift up your voice and shout for joy.

"What a friend we have in Jesus," and how much we need just such a friend I think you know. You may not have another, but He is always your friend. He made you, and understands you, He loves you though sin has marred you and left its ugly scars. The "daughters of music" have been silent too long.

If our life is dark and cheerless we cannot hope to attract others. We must not look at ourselves too much. If we look unto Him that is mighty to save even to the uttermost them that believe, then a new song shall be put into our hearts.

Then as Luther says, "Joy will be the color of our emblem." And Jesus said, "No one shall take your joy from you."

"Look at yourself," says the devil. You cringe before him, wondering if you have enough energy remaining in your faith to point to the cross. That cross will solve the problems posed by the evil one. "Look unto Jesus, the author and finisher of faith" and you shall have power supplied to meet all your needs. You will be glad too.

Chapter 6

"My God, How Wonderful Thou Art"

And there were certain Greeks among them that came up to worship at the feast.

The same came therefore to Philip, which was of Bethsaida of Galilee, and desired him, saying, Sir, we would see Jesus.

Philip cometh and telleth Andrew: and again Andrew and Philip tell Jesus.

And Jesus answered them, saying, The hour is come, that the Son of man should be glorified.

Verily, verily, I say unto you, Except a corn of wheat fall into the ground and die, it abideth alone: but if it die, it bringeth forth much fruit.

He that loveth his life shall lose it; and he that hateth his life in this world shall keep it unto life eternal.

If any man serve me, let him follow me; and where I am, there shall also my servant be: if any man serve me, him will my Father honour.

Now is my soul troubled; and what shall I say? Father, save me from this hour: but for this cause came I unto this hour.

Father, glorify thy name. Then came there a voice from heaven, saying, I have both glorified it, and will glorify it again.

The people therefore, that stood by, and heard it, said that it thundered: others said, An angel spake to him.

Jesus answered and said, This voice came not because of me, but for your sakes.

Now is the judgment of this world: now shall the prince of this world be cast out.

And, I, if I be lifted up from the earth, will draw all men unto me.

This he said, signifying what death he should die.

John 12:20-33

THE Greeks who came to Jerusalem for the great feast, give expression to the deepest longing found in the heart of the human race. "We would see Jesus." Call the longing whatever you please. It may be a longing for peace, happiness, contentment—or just Jesus. The human heart hungers with an undying need for just that which Jesus can supply. The incessant tears, sacrifices, altars, and temples, rude or artistic, indicate for us how real the longing must be. Everywhere you hear the crying. Human philosophies have done their best, but the heart is still crying. So with the cultured Greeks.

Just who these men and what their names were, matters little. The important thing is that they had come to see Jesus. Strange that at the very beginning of His life, while He was yet a babe in the manger, wise men from the East came to see

Him and here at the close of His ministry, the Greeks who were cultured Gentiles came to see Him. From the North and the South, from the East and the West they came—God bless them all.

The presence of these Greeks at the temple was significant and Jesus at once catches the full force of the event. To Him it was a sure token too of the fruit of that death. So far very little had been done for the Gentile world. They were not excluded, however, for even Solomon in his dedication prayer remembered them. In Israel, prophet after prophet arose to proclaim the will of God, but none entered upon the highways and byways of the Gentile world. Jesus once said, "I am not sent but to the lost sheep of the house of Israel." The prophets did foretell the time when the Gentiles should come to the light of the Messiah. On several occasions Jesus extended His help to those who were not of the Hebrew people. The woman of Canaan who pleaded for her daughter and the centurion of Capernaum are illustrious examples of the kingdom kindness extended to the Gentiles. The dawn of a new day when the spiritual economies should belong to them was not far distant.

The Jews of the dispersion living in the scattered countries, carried the Scriptures with them. They already had been translated into Greek. And thus the preparation was made. Then too, there was in the Gentile heart a secret longing for something they did not possess. They were reaching out to find it. In spite of the numberless deities they had not found God. The apostle Paul found an altar inscribed to "the unknown God" which tells the story of a fruitless search. But it is also reasonable to assume that many Greeks, because of their contact with the Jews, were somewhat familiar with the Scriptures and were quietly saying, "We would see Jesus." What a rich fruitage would mature here when the Gospel seed is sown. But Jesus must first suffer and die or there would be no full Gospel to proclaim. That's why He was touched so when these strange visitors asked to see Him.

Did these Greeks see Him? We are not told, but I believe they did. The heart of Jesus was so big that it included these men too—He could not disappoint them when they had come seeking Him.

"The hour is come that the Son of man shall be glorified." His own people had not glorified Him. "He came to his own and his own received him not." They not only rejected Him but persecuted Him at every opportunity. Most of His disciples "walked no more with him." But He saw the beginning of a new era, and there inseparably associated with that era was the awful thought of death. "Now is my soul troubled, and what shall I say? Father, save me from this hour, but for this cause came I unto this hour." He is to be glorified in His death. "Verily, I say unto you, Except a corn of wheat fall into the ground and die, it abideth alone, but if it die it bringeth forth much fruit."

Now in nature death is always a condition of fruitfulness. Here is a grain of wheat. The mystery of life sleeps within it. But to bring forth fruit it must be cast into the earth and die. The dormant life within is awakened when the outer form is broken. Without this process it must remain alone. Science has demonstrated that cell life reproduces in the same way. Christ enunciated a law that is universal.

Death was a condition of fruitfulness in Christ too. "When I am lifted up I will draw all men unto me." His death would not terminate but germinate His work. He had already done some great works—removed distress and disease, transformed men and set them to thinking, and communicated a mass of truth to all who listened. And yet how meager the results had been. How little His own friends understood, until after His death, what He meant when He said, "It is expedient for you that I go away."

His death opened the heart of God and, what is more, it opened wide the world. The message of the reconciliation wrought by His death was destined to reach the whole world. He could see the progress of the Kingdom. He saw men go out in the power of His might everywhere to proclaim the Gospel and to establish churches builded upon that truth. "When his soul is made an offering for sin, he shall see his seed," so says the prophet Isaiah for he too had visions of what was to be. How vast has been the fruit of Jesus' death.

Seed produces fruit of its kind. So Christ produces men like Himself—Christ men, cross men are the product. How much fruit has been borne by that death we cannot know until we gaze in breathless wonder upon the ransomed hosts before the throne of God.

Death to self is the condition of fruitfulness in our spiritual life. If life is used only for ourselves —the gratification of our own desires—we abide alone. Much alone. We lose life that way. When we are gone then all is gone. But if we give of our life to others, we not only preserve it for ourselves but it is multiplied in the lives of others.

What a price Jesus was asked to pay, that we might live. If He had spared Himself the way would never have been prepared. But Jesus is thinking too of what it will cost the disciple to be faithful. Where He goes we will follow. It will be a way of utter self-denial. Does that seem hard, then remember the other way is harder. Even Moses knew that, for didn't he say he would "rather suffer affliction with the people of God than enjoy the pleasures of sin for a season, esteeming the reproach of Christ greater riches." The company of Jesus will compensate abundantly for any renunciation we may be called upon to make.

"Father, glorify thy name," prayed Jesus, and the heavens thundered at the thought of the great sacrifice about to be made and a voice out of heaven said, "I have glorified it and will glorify it again."

Oh, for a greater vision of God. "We would see Jesus." Isaiah saw the glory of Jehovah in the temple—to Simon Peter it came while he was employed in the fishing smack—to Joan of Arc it came in the little rude kitchen—and to Martin Luther while he gazed upon a few simple words of Scripture. To the wisemen from the East it came while they worshipped at the manger—to the Greeks when they found Jesus in the temple. And today we behold Him surrounded by the glory of the ages and we see Him as "the only begotten of the Father, full of grace and truth." Jesus is the supreme manifestation of God. Get your New Testament open again. Gaze on Jesus as He moves among men in His wearisome journey from the cradle to the cross and the open grave. "There is your vision—you shall see no more. But be sure you see all there is to see." See the men and the women, the multitudes for whom He died—see the ransomed hosts past and present who prostrate themselves before Him to sing their song of adora-

tion. You can see God everywhere. You can see
man's need everywhere. You can catch a glimpse
of His plan everywhere. "Draw back the curtains
and there you see God." He is speaking to all who
will listen.

> My God, how wonderful Thou art,
> Thy majesty how bright,
> How beautiful Thy mercy seat
> In depths of burning light.
>
> How wonderful, how beautiful
> The sight of Thee must be.
> Thine endless wisdom, boundless power,
> And awful purity.
>
> Yet I may love Thee too, O Lord!
> Almighty as Thou art,
> For Thou hast stooped to ask of me
> The love of my poor heart.

Chapter 7

Gethsemanes in Miniature

And he came out, and went, as he was wont, to the mount of Olives; and his disciples also followed him.

And when he was at the place, he said unto them, Pray that ye enter not into temptation.

And he was withdrawn from them about a stone's cast, and kneeled down, and prayed,

Saying, Father, if thou be willing, remove this cup from me: nevertheless not my will, but thine, be done.

And there appeared an angel unto him from heaven, strengthening him.

Luke 22:39-43

JESUS in Gethsemane. Was there ever any sorrow comparable to the one endured by our Savior here? Was there ever a burden so hard to be borne as the one that lay upon Him when He grovelled in Gethsemane? Was there ever anyone so lonely as when He drank that cup of anguish amid the moaning olive trees that cast about Him the flickering, haunting shadows—a portent of the lonely death upon the cross? The way from Gethsemane to Calvary, the highest hill in all the world, tested the spirit of the Son of God. No one seemed to understand—nor could anyone fathom the depths of His sorrow when He became our great sin bearer—when as the Lamb of God He entered the sanctuary, and the sins of the world— yours and mine—were poured out upon Him.

Then and there was thrust upon Him the darkest, the most utter loneliness ever known, while He pours out His heart to God in pleadings and supplications that must have wrenched the heart of the Father. Over and over again He prays that the cup might be removed from Him. The prospect seems to overwhelm Him momentarily, but He always adds, "Not my will, but Thine be done." How could He avoid the issue for which He had been appointed and sent? Here, I think, more than upon any other occasion, His human nature recoils. Nor is that to be wondered at for He was as human as any child born of the race. But when the pain of soul seems to become unbearable and His anguish so unspeakable that beads of perspiration become blood and His very life is threatened, the Father sends an angel to comfort Him and the Son of God our sin bearer emerges from His Gethsemane rendezvous a strengthened soul, refreshed and invigorated for the Calvary scenes, oppressive as these were. He is not afraid. "An angel came and comforted him."

Thus it had been at the beginning of His ministry too, when after the great trials the angels came and ministered to Him in the wilderness. And accompanying Him through the joys and sorrows of His toil had been legions of angels who stood ready to answer His beck and call. And now at the end of the way an angel bearing comfort and encouragement comes to refresh and strengthen the suffering Savior.

Yes, He was divine, but, oh, how real was His suffering. He had so much—but oh, how much He needed, for eternal destinies were bound up with His experience there, only a stone's throw from three beloved and weary disciples. The day had been too much for them—Jesus must bear the burden in loneliness.

We love to turn again and again to the lonely scene at Gethsemane and each time we learn something more of the great love revealed there. To understand His boundless compassion—to touch only the hem of His garment—means a better understanding of life and all its problems. It helps make us strong for the Gethsemanes through which we must pass—for we all have our Gethsemanes, agonies in miniature to be sure, for there could be no other like unto the one which He knew.

There is the Gethsemane of sin. When we come to know sin and its nature and its consequences we are anguish-filled. Sin is rebellion against God— enmity toward One who has been kind and good to us. When we learn to know that sin in its final consequence works our ultimate and eternal separation from God, then anxious fears must overwhelm. How could it be otherwise? How often you and I have sinned against God and done that which is evil in His sight. And no burden is more real than the one imposed by a wide-awake consciousness of our guilt. Then it is blessed to look unto Gethsemane where Jesus really assumed the guilt and the burden of our sin, for it is written, "Behold the Lamb of God, which taketh away the sin of the world."

Then there is a Gethsemane of loneliness. How unspeakably lonely we sometimes become. We may struggle with some real problem or disappointment, or we may be overwhelmed by bereavement and affliction. There seem to be some things that we cannot share with anyone because no one can fully understand. They may understand their own sorrows, but ours are hidden. Thus we move along slowly and silently under the shadows of an indefinable loneliness. Then we remember that our Lord and Savior was the loneliest of all men and that He entered into the agonies of Gethsemane that "he might be tried in all things like as we are." He will understand though no one else can, and we need "fear no ill, with Him at hand to bless." Alone and yet not alone. How that paradox has helped lonely hearts.

Great sorrows have opened many a way into Gethsemane. You may have been spared. Certain it is that not all have suffered alike. But how remote is the hope that we should be spared the sorrows which belong to the common lot of man. Today you are seeking to share the sorrow of someone who has been afflicted—seeking to make the burden a little lighter for them. There are times and occasions when the burden of sorrow seems oppressively cruel. You want to be of some help—you want to walk a mile or two with them and commiserate as you go. Tomorrow the occasion may be reversed and others will walk with you. May those who walk with you when your spirits are low be able to tell you the story of Jesus in Gethsemane again.

How little we calculate the sorrows that are to be. We are grateful to God that He has so made us that we do not anticipate every pain. But when affliction comes, be the sorrow ever so searching, we will look unto Jesus, the man of sorrows who knew Gethsemane so well.

An angel was sent from heaven to comfort Jesus in His trial and the angels of God are watching over you. Angels are real—helpers sent from God.

As little children we prayed to God that the angel who guided us during the day, might also care for us at night. Blessed childhood, blessed memories. A little prayer and we sank into blissful slumber because the angels of God surrounded us.

Chapter 8

The Circumstances
Are Grim

And it came to pass, that as he was come nigh unto Jericho, a certain blind man sat by the way side begging:

And hearing the multitude pass by, he asked what it meant.

And they told him, that Jesus of Nazareth passeth by.

And he cried, saying, Jesus, thou son of David, have mercy on me.

And they which went before rebuked him, that he should hold his peace: but he cried so much the more, Thou son of David, have mercy on me.

And Jesus stood, and commanded him to be brought unto him: and when he was come near, he asked him,

Saying, What wilt thou that I shall do unto thee? And he said, Lord, that I may receive my sight.

And Jesus said unto him, Receive thy sight: thy faith hath saved thee.

And immediately he received his sight, and followed him, glorifying God: and all the people, when they saw it, gave praise unto God.

Luke 18:35-43

THIS is the pathetic story of a blind man who chanced to meet Jesus when the Son of man was on His way to Jerusalem where He would be called upon to face circumstances as grim as death. Jesus knew that the Scriptures concerning the suffering Servant were about to be fulfilled. He had sought for some time to prepare the disciples to face that issue. This journey through Jericho to Jerusalem would not soon be forgotten by these Galilean fishermen who for three years had clung so closely to Jesus of Nazareth. The fact that they did not understand the things that were transpiring only fixed the events more firmly in their memories. And whether or not they understood the whys and wherefores of all that Jesus did, they felt they owed Him and determined to give Him a loyalty devoted even to prison and to death. Jesus was moved by a strange, lonely spirit that day on the way to Jerusalem and the disciples were fearful that something terrible was about to happen. Their hearts within them trembled. What a retinue it was that plodded through the dusty roads to the ancient city that day. Men who knew every nook and niche and bay in Galilee, but for whom the city held ominous fear. They watched every movement of Jesus, their all in all. Jesus in all His majestic beauty, crowned with a lowly humility which made His loneliness stand out boldly, leads the procession. Can you follow them as they slowly move along? No, they will not desert Him though the way be dark and the paths be studded with mystery. On to Jerusalem will they follow, come what may. Undying devotion and heroic loyalty would not permit them to think or plan otherwise. Is there no one who will see as they do? In the motley crowd that surges the approaches to Jericho, is there no one who will see beneath the peasant garb of Jesus a glory that must be divine? Yes, even on the way to His crucifixion, Jesus has prepared some incidents that would bolster their faltering faith and help make them stronger when the time of testing came.

Strange, isn't it, that a blind man should be the first to sense the glory of the approaching Savior. Bartimeus, a blind beggar who had sat at the gates of Jericho begging gifts from those who came and from those who left its portals, cried saying, "Jesus thou Son of David have mercy upon me." He cried so loud and attracted so much attention that some of the disciples really were embarrassed. They asked him to hold his peace, but he somehow sensed the invisible glory and knew that the opportunity of his life-time had come, so he only cried the more loudly. When need becomes acute, it has the momentum and the courage to make itself known. And no need ever presented itself to Jesus which was not given immediate attention. Bartimeus' cry of faith touched

Jesus and the divine Redeemer reached out saying, "Receive thy sight, thy faith hath made thee
whole." The incident created a deep impression
upon all the people and they praised God for it.
For Jesus and His unlettered, weather-beaten fishermen the incident must have provided a much
needed respite from a wearisome loneliness that
dogged their way to the holy city.

And do you think that the blind man ever forgot the experiences of that day in Jericho? A new
day dawned for him and as he received his sight,
Jesus of Nazareth, the Son of David, became his
king and Lord. And if the people who saw it
praised God for the kindness visited upon Bartimeus, *"his life* was changed into an endless song
of praise."

And in the same day Jesus met Zaccheus in
Jericho and be sure he never forgot the day. Blessed experiences came upon him and his household
when Jesus entered and abode in his home. Hearts
that trusted Jesus always became glad. Others who
saw Jesus that day sensed that he had strange and
marvelous powers, but when Zaccheus saw Him
he knew that He was the King of glory. Others
were embarrassed, amazed, and inspired, but
Zaccheus knew that his life through and through
had been changed by His presence. He was a new
creature with new standards, new ideals, and
within him was born an eternal hope.

Matthew was "sitting in the seat of custom" when the call came to him. Do you think he ever forgot the day when Jesus spoke to him? The transformation effected that day carried through and from that day on the "destiny of Matthew the publican was wrapped up in the kingdom of God."

Maybe you think the Samaritan woman could forget. She had conversed with the Messiah when she came to draw water from Jacob's well near Sychar. Others had seen Him too but observed nothing unusual, but for her thenceforth He was all in all. She became a great witness. The folks at Sychar learned to know Him because she testified. The consequences were far-reaching because she transformed the incident into an opportunity.

Thus Jesus blessed many who were willing to listen. Not because their measure of faith was so great but because they believed enough to ask His aid and in granting that He increased their faith. The cry of faith, no matter how faint, was never unheeded by Jesus. Can you recall a single incident where Jesus refused to assist because the faith was too weak? Was He ever too busy to touch a bleeding heart or to mend a broken body?

Wherever Jesus went, some soul was sent rejoicing on its way. In the cities, in the country, in the highways and the byways—everywhere was the hand of Jesus extended to help. He asked no compensation, He claimed no reward, He only loved to the uttermost, to the end of limitless love.

Even for the social outcasts Jesus cared. The publicans and sinners despised by the Jews, found a place in His heart. He came to help those who needed help. "They that be whole need not a physician, but they that are sick." And the outcasts found in Him the greatest friend. He never condoned sin, yet for the sinner He always had a place. How big must that heart have been to enfold so many.

Others would have helped many in need but they could not. Only Jesus *could* help. He knew the needs both of body and soul and He possessed the power commensurate with every need. "Nothing is impossible with God." He could mend a body broken by disease but He could also save the soul. No matter how devastating were the conditions of misery, no matter how hopeless things appeared, Jesus could find a way out. "He alone can make straight the crooked things of life." He helped when the spark of faith was very dim and hardly recognizable as faith, for He so often said, "Thy faith hath saved thee." Much or little, learned or ignorant—He accepted the faith that prompted men to ask for aid.

It is evident that Jesus saw the good, saw the possibilities in man. The searcher of hearts could

discern the thoughts, the aims, and the hopes that
were lodged there. We see man only in the rough
exterior, the Master looks at the heart and sees
a ransomed soul. "Men saw in John Bunyan only
a cursing drunken tinker, but God saw the poten-
tialities, and He wove into the life of Bunyan the
fabric of *Pilgrim's Progress.* Ordinary trades
people saw in Dwight L. Moody only a small
business man, but God saw the great evangelist."
Men saw Augustine and turned their faces from
him because he was a dissipated youth who ruined
his own soul and broke the heart of his mother,
but God saw him cleansed from his sin and re-
leased from his errors and gave him a fitting place
within the church during a critical age. Men saw
me and all my sin—and these were abhorrent—and
they could see no more. No future, no hope, no
redemption. But God saw my longing and my
heart's desire and He recreated me so that "all
things are become new." Hands that once were
nailed to the cross enveloped me and I found rest
there in the everlasting arms. You may be sure
that He cares whether anyone else does or not.

And in the kingdom men by grace are saved to
serve. Even though we become the children of
God we cannot do all things, but something there
is that we can do. Some little area of service will
be given to us. We may not be expected to write a
Gospel as Matthew did, but we can sing a song for

Him, or maybe say a word to someone who will listen.

> If you are too weak to journey
> Up the mountain steep and high,
> You can stand within the valley,
> As the multitudes go by.
> You can chant a happy measure
> As they slowly move along.
> Though they may forget the singer
> They will not forget the song.

We are in the midst of another Lent and the spirit of the season is Christ. We meet Him again and again in all His glory, in His humanity and in His divinity. Beautiful Savior, King of creation, come and touch my weary soul. Just a prayer for His presence and He will come, not to call, but to abide. Many will see Him but He will only be passing by. They will emerge from Lent without any special blessings because they didn't recognize Him. He was ready to bless but they were not ready to receive. Too bad. Lord help us to say with Bartimeus, "Thou Son of David, have mercy upon me." And He will pause to lay His hand upon the drooping shoulders and say, "Thy faith hath saved thee." What faith? Mine, of course. It isn't much but it is a voice calling for Jesus, a hand reaching out for help. God never turns away from anyone who sincerely seeks His help.

Chapter 9

Too Good to Be True

Now upon the first day of the week, very early in the morning, they came unto the sepulchre, bringing the spices which they had prepared, and certain others with them.

And they found the stone rolled away from the sepulchre.

And they entered in, and found not the body of the Lord Jesus.

And it came to pass, as they were much perplexed thereabout, behold, two men stood by them in shining garments:

And as they were afraid, and bowed down their faces to the earth, they said unto them, Why seek ye the living among the dead?

He is not here, but is risen: remember how he spake unto you when he was yet in Galilee,

Saying, The Son of man must be delivered into the hands of sinful men, and be crucified, and the third day rise again.

And they remembered his words,

And returned from the sepulchre, and told all these things unto the eleven, and to all the rest.   Luke 24:1-9

EASTER DAY has burst forth in a ray of glory dawning after a night of weeping. How much of wonder and joy are bound up in that word "Resurrection." Life becomes different—is altogether altered—when viewed in the light of the Easter day message, proclaimed by the angel at the open grave. What a consummation *that* was, after a week of such tragic sorrow. Tremulous wonder, inadequate and blundering speech, which tries so hard and yet cannot convey the richness and the fulness of its glory. Thank God for Easter which crowned the Son of God with victory. "He was declared to be the Son of God with power by the resurrection from the dead."

Let us arise and sing together the traditional Easter song, which has for generations past given expression to the joys created by the day. As our forefathers have sung, from Muskego to the cathedral-like structures of today, so let us sing:

> He is arisen! Glorious word!
> Now reconciled is God, my Lord;
> The gates of heaven are open.
> My Jesus died triumphantly
> And Satan's arrows broken lie,
> Destroyed hell's direst weapon.
> Oh, hear! What cheer!
> Christ victorious riseth glorious,
> Life He giveth—
> He was dead, but see, He liveth.

Many fail to accept the Easter proclamation because it is too wonderful—it is too extravagant in its claims and in its promises. How often we have heard people say, "It is too good to be true." If that is generally true it is more particularly true in the kingdom of God which is so different, so unique and indescribably excellent. So much is paraded that is fraud and deception, that one is loath to believe a thing so superlatively good. Too much light may blind as will darkness. The disciples were bewildered and were the first to doubt. It is written of them, "They believed not for joy." It was too good to be true. Pain may grip the heart when one is glad, just as much as when one is sad. You sometimes have seen people weep for joy. Joy, like sadness, is confusing. Evidence that should bring peace arouses unbelief momentarily.

Many a doubt has arisen in sheer joy. We were very seriously ill, but those who stood by, wondering and praying said, "He has passed the crisis." Could it be true? You were entering the valley of shadows and then suddenly there was a turn for the better. Was it true? And our joy almost overwhelms our faith. The soldiers asked on Armistice Day—"Can it be possible, is the war really over?" It is too good to be true. We are frightened to believe some things that are terrible, but we are almost as slow at believing things that are joyous.

In the spiritual realm the same conditions prevail. The tragic and the glorious elements in our faith both raise questions of doubt. "We question the warnings because they are terrible and we doubt the promises because they are too gracious." Men would like to eliminate hell because the thought of it is awful—and then on the other hand isn't heaven too unspeakably beautiful? The spirit of doubt and hesitation is preeminent in spiritual things. The spirit of falsehood obscures the vision. "The god of this world hath blinded the minds of them which believe not." In the material world we demand scientific proof to establish credibility. In the spiritual world no such proofs are available. Wouldn't it seem impossible that a bird could carry itself in mid air? Yes, but you have seen a bird and you know that it can be done. I hold in my hand a little flower seed. Could it ever be anything but a seed? Yes, there is life within it, and as incredible as it may seem that seed will clothe itself with vestments many-colored and beautiful. That truth has been demonstrated beyond any doubt. Every Easter lily is a miracle.

There are a lot of things that are hard to believe. My grandparents used to drive a yoke of oxen from our little village in southern Wisconsin, all the way to Milwaukee, about ninety miles distant, to deliver their wheat. It took them about ten days to make the trip. They were doing well then. They would never have believed that the same trip could be made by airplane while mother prepared the dinner meal. When our grandparents came from Europe they made the trip by sailing vessel and the trip required anywhere from six to twelve weeks. They would never have believed it possible that present day liners could make the same trip in about five days. Men and women of that generation suffering excruciating pains, the result of injury or disease, would never have believed possible the miracles of surgery performed today under the various types of anesthetics. They would have said, "That would be fine. But— it's too good to be true." When dentists began with the process called nerve blocking, the little boy who anticipated much pain, said, "That can't be; that is really too good to be true." So is man. We must see and touch and prove a thing to establish its credibility.

In the field of Christian experience our doubting natures immediately call into question the most satisfying and thrilling truths, simply because the promise is too great. And yet, thank God, we are not willing to yield our faith in it, but we lose much of the joy which it otherwise would provide us. That same question arises about the whole "economy of grace." Can it be that God would seek out lost and condemned humanity that He might freely pour out to them His cup of goodness? Will the Easter message cause us less difficulty than it did the disciples of whom it is written, "They believed not for joy"?

Have you ever thought how thankful we ought to be that we may believe in a God who is good, a God whom we may call our Father? Let these words in our creed never be uttered lightly: "I believe in God the Father Almighty." That is a wonderful truth and it brings a like assurance. One is over us who is omnipotent; He is guided by inherent wisdom and unfailing goodness. His vigil is and will be sleepless and eternal. Can you think of anything that would be more comforting or more assuring? Sometimes when that faith really takes hold of our hearts we are constrained to say, "Can that really be true?"

Yes, God is a gracious heavenly Father with whom we may rest in peace and security. No harm can come to us if we trust in Him. The children of men cry for Him and for the comfort that He alone can confer. Oh, how men longed that He would come out of His spirit world, reveal Himself and live with them. This is the cry, "Show us the Father, and it sufficeth us." So He did exactly that. He revealed Himself through Jesus Christ as a God of love, who came "to seek and to save the lost." He did live with men, He talked with them, helped them at every turn and then pressed His love and His care to such extremity that He died for them. "How unsearchable are his riches and his ways past finding out." Can it be? Yes, that is true for that is what the Word of God teaches.

The incarnation—we cannot understand it. Voices will say, "Can it be true?" Did God take upon Himself the form of man and become obedient even unto death? Yes!

No wonder that the disciples after the crucifixion went back to their old occupations. What else was there for them to do? Such a situation didn't yield to reason. The cross was the end—the finis had been accomplished. Perhaps they had been fooled many times before. The less they said about the whole matter the less would be the ridicule. Not strange at all, that when Jesus appeared after His resurrection they were almost overwhelmed. They thought a spectre had appeared. For they had seen people die, they had seen them buried. "They believed not for joy." That one who was so dead, that a spear could be thrust into His side and water and blood issue from the wound —that He could be alive again was too much for them. Could that be true? Thomas said he wouldn't believe unless he could lay his hand in the wound in Jesus' side and lay his finger on the wound in His hand. When that opportunity came, Thomas no longer doubted. He fell down before Jesus worshipping Him and saying much in a few words, "My Lord and my God."

We are staggered by the Easter message. It is the greatest message ever proclaimed to man. Maybe we will have to say, "Lord I believe, help thou mine unbelief." That message is a good message but it is not too good to be true. "I know that my Redeemer liveth—and because He lives I too shall live."

There have been and still are those who deny the resurrection. Rationalism has sought in every generation to destroy that faith. That denial is as old as unbelief. But the battering rams of unbelief have only helped to establish more firmly still the resurrection hope. Let the world do its worst. It is still true that Christ arose from the dead. "He lives and reigns to all eternity." Peter, Paul, and John, and all the builders of the kingdom staked everything on that fact. The church was founded and has prospered upon it. The New Testament is vibrant with the assurance that Christ arose from the dead. He was the firstfruits—we shall follow.

The hope of a life after death is not an iridescent dream—it is not wishful thinking—it is not too good to be true. It is for you and me a star of hope. Take that away and we have remaining only the impenetrable gloom of the grave. Take the resurrection Christ out of our plan of salvation and the church builded for Him must collapse.

Thank God we believe in the Easter message!

Chapter 10

Instinct, Longing, and Need

If a man die, shall he live again? all the days of my appointed time will I wait, till my change come.

Job 14:14

HAVE you asked that question? Job asked it, and the ages have been absorbed by it. Immortality has been an important element in all religions—pagan and Christian alike. The Buddhists have made their inquiries and the followers of Mohammed have asked. Men of every faith have showed a deep concern about that which follows after death. Men of all faiths, men who have no faith at all, infidels and agnostics, have spent themselves in protracted discussions of this question which is of such vital concern.

What you believe about the answer to that question, "If a man die, shall he live again," is going to make a lot of difference to you. Your attitudes, your convictions, will be determined by it. Is this life all or is it "but a vestibule"? When you die are you snuffed out like a candle, or does something in you survive the apparent "limitations of time and space"? Is death an eternal sleep or can we say, "There is no death, what seems so is transition"?

Christianity from its early beginnings has given a very definite affirmative answer to the question. Generations upon generations have repeated the historic confession, "I believe in life everlasting." Our greatest institutions have been founded upon that assurance. Beautiful oratorios have proclaimed *that* life, art has sought by its most sacred efforts to depict it, and the greatest philosophies of all ages have been guided by it. No misgivings ever troubled those who rested in it. If the consummation is glorious, what if the way be rugged here?

In recent years rationalism has again assailed the doctrine of immortality by insisting upon its incredibility. "Yesterday we were here, tomorrow we shall not be"—that is their conclusion. Now that is not a new philosophy but one as old as the hills. And it is a poor philosophy to live by. What if we can't explain the processes involved in the resurrection. Are we to believe only the obvious? Then science and philosophy indeed would be in a perilous state. Mathematics is filled with assumptions, and yet we trust its correctness. How many understand Einstein's theory of relativity? No one seems to understand that and yet it is freely discussed in newspapers and magazines. When Einstein read these dissertations maybe he too was baffled. Every day we are assuming things more difficult to believe than the doctrine of immortality. Science and philosophy do not, cannot, deny the origin of life though they have not been able to understand it. Why then should they question the possibility of its continuation?

The resurrection of Jesus and the empty grave give us the one great comforting assurance that we need. And the watchword of the Christian Church will always be, "Because He lives, I too shall live."

However, there are three very telling arguments which support and substantiate the Christian belief in immortality. Let us look at these for a few moments.

What about man's instinct, for there is in every man an inborn sense of a higher destiny than this world. Man may be groping, but that much he feels. That's instinct. You have seen the robins disappear before the onset of winter and you have waited for their return when spring came. They are guided by instinct. The homing pigeon carries a message attached to a foot, carries it over an uncharted course of hundreds of miles and falls exhausted at its destination. The swallow according to some authorities makes its return in the spring on the same date, year after year. The muskrat gathers her materials and builds her home in the swamp because winter is coming, guided by the shelter instinct. The beaver cuts his tree and then builds a bridge to cross the rapids. And never does instinct lead astray or misdirect. Do you think that God who is infinitely good would create us and inspire us by these holy instincts—write into our hearts the hope of immortality, and then at the end disappoint us? That would be inconsistent with the character of God. Why do I have the sense of smell? Because there are things to smell —odors that destroy and fragrance that pleases. Why have I been blessed with the sense of hearing? Because there are things to hear, words and music that will please the soul, words that may warn when danger is near. Why do I have the sense of touch and taste? Because there are things to touch and things to taste. God has not created a faculty that is useless. What of man's longing for life eternal? The answer is: There must be a life eternal to enjoy, else why the longing?

Then on the other hand we have man's longing for eternity to reckon with. And that didn't come with the kingdom of God. Man has always longed for life eternal. The Egyptians who lived three thousand years before Christ was born, believed in and longed for a life after death. Old weathered inscriptions tell the story. Greek philosophers gave much time and thought to the question. Incidents dating back to the time of Plato still survive. Men hastened life and brought on an early death because they wanted to live forever. Humanity has always needed the refreshing and reviving hope of a life after death. No country anywhere, however remote; no race anywhere, however savage, cruel, and ignorant it may have been,—but that this longing has occupied a large place in their religious aspirations.

Isn't it reasonable to assume that this persistent, universal longing has its origin in God? God made man and He endowed him with this faculty. "Every *natural* longing has its satisfaction." Is the soul filled with a hunger that God must disappoint? That does not seem very likely.

Immortality also represents man's greatest need. It is a reasonable inference that this fragmentary life will somewhere find completion and perfection. Possibilities are so infinite, yet the time allotted here is so short. One feels that even the greatest intellects have only scratched the surface. Artists have sought to sketch what they in vision saw, but only a relatively small part of what they saw ever touched the canvas. Great musicians despair of reproducing the masterpieces that have surged through their soul. But there must be a time and an occasion when God will permit great souls to finish that which they have begun. If death ends all, suicide would be the best way out for a great many people. Humanity needs another sphere in which justice shall prevail. Tyrants shall not always be enthroned, neither shall the saints forever languish in the tombs. "Vice shall not always wear the purple nor shall virtue always be clothed in rags." Nero, the ruthless emperor, beheads Paul. Only in the life which is to be can such cruel injustice ever be righted. God plans well and eventually His plans will be apparent. But the adjustment will not be made here: that is evident. No matter how we look at it, man needs eternity. A denial of life immortal will destroy the faith that makes a good life really possible. The consciousness that we are destined for greater things helps raise us up and gives us the support we need.

"Is it possible that the tree shall outlive the man who planted it, the garment outlast the man that made it? Is it possible that Tennyson's 'In Memoriam' should be immortal, and immortality be denied the man who wrote it? Is it possible and reasonable that Savonarola, Wyclif, Huss, and all the slaughtered saints should die a martyr's death and not receive a martyr's crown? Is it possible that Nero and Diocletian could wade in innocent blood and not suffer for their crimes? Shall the

Son of God be crucified but not be exalted?" These pertinent sentences which appeared in a published sermon some time ago, are certainly worth remembering. The more you think about man's instinct, his longing, and his need, the more reasonable and satisfying does the doctrine of immortality become.

When we turn to the Word of God, Job's question is very definitely answered and the matter is settled so far as the Christian is concerned. The Word of God is final and with it the evidence is conclusive. Read the parable of the rich man and Lazarus and be forever satisfied that the vital question, "If a man die, shall he live again?" is answered for all. Read again the thrilling story of Jesus' resurrection and what John and Paul said about it and be forever comforted. My dear God and heavenly Father, when the way is dark and the burdens are oppressive and the spirits are low and discouraged, draw aside the veil a bit and let me see the things that are to be, and I shall be comforted.

Thanks, Jesus, that Thou hast "brought life and immortality to light."

Chapter 11

Let Us Keep the Feast

*Moreover when ye fast, be not, as the hypocrites, of
a sad countenance: for they disfigure their faces, that
they may appear unto men to fast. Verily I say unto you,
They have their reward.*

*But thou, when thou fastest, anoint thine head, and
wash thy face;*

*That thou appear not unto men to fast, but unto thy
Father which is in secret: and thy Father, which seeth
in secret, shall reward thee openly.* Matthew 6:16-18

*And when one of them that sat at meat with him
heard these things, he said unto him, Blessed is he that
shall eat bread in the kingdom of God.* Luke 14:15

WE are entering another season of Lent. We
cannot avoid the issues. We must face them
bravely and squarely.

To be true to her call and to maintain her commission the Church *must* speak the truth. It will

be essential again to tell the people why Lent is necessary. It will also be the responsibility of the church, again to tell the people of the remedy which God has provided against sin. We are standing with our backs to the wall and there can be no hedging. The times are tragic and we are concerned about the outcome. Never before has the darkness been more impenetrable. May God in His gracious and infinite mercy lead the way, and the ultimate issue and consummation will be good, however impossible the night may seem.

Both the elements that make Lent so important —the need and the remedy—are hard to acknowledge, because both are to our everlasting shame and discredit. The one because it reflects the evil within us, the other because it exposes our utter helplessness.

For a long period of years it has been customary to observe Lent in the Lutheran Church. The observance may have changed somewhat in character, may have been altered in its intensity, but some recognition has been given to this season.

I wonder if we really appreciate the full significance and meaning of Lent and its observance. What kind of definition would you give for Lent? Someone might ask you about it. Could we give a definite and understandable answer? We know that it is a period on our church calendar which lasts about six weeks and that it is followed by

Easter morning and the resurrection story. We know that during Lent there are special services planned and announced weeks before they are held. It's a time in which we are asked to give more time to meditation and Bible study, to intensify our prayer life. It is a time in which to recapitulate and commemorate the sufferings of our Lord and Savior, which reach their climax on Good Friday when He is nailed to the Roman cross on Calvary.

> I take, O cross, thy shadow
> For my abiding place;
> I ask no other sunshine than
> The sunshine of His face;
> Content to let the world go by,
> To know no gain or loss,
> My sinful self my only shame,
> My glory all the cross.

There is in the observance of Lent a place for fasting and a place for feasting. Under the guidance of God's Spirit it is your privilege to assign to each of these functions what fits your own conditions best.

Lent is not divinely appointed. We are not told that we must observe it. But whether we observe it or not is going to make a great deal of difference. The atonement, our convictions, and our faith are all so sacred that a calm and prayerful study of them all should create a need, establish our faith, and make us stronger. There will be hard times ahead, days of testing when the recollection of the Lenten observance may mean the difference between victory and defeat. We must be careful not to stress the fast and miss the feast.

It is entirely scriptural, and what is more, it is entirely practical to fast. The Christian church from the very beginning has employed fasting, to give expression to a great need and also through the same channel to be refreshed. To abstain from certain foods, and to refrain from some things, innocent in themselves, for the sake of becoming more deeply spiritual, to employ more time for our own spiritual devotion, must of course be a beneficial program. To deny oneself in order that we may better remember our Savior is a spiritual devotion much to be desired. But to abstain from eating or to refrain from certain common pleasures cannot merit the gift of salvation. It merits nothing, it earns nothing, it only helps make us more receptive to God's wondrous gifts. Salvation is full and free without fasting. Fasting does not even make us more worthy, it only opens a way through which God may shower His gifts upon us. The trouble with too many who fast is this: they believe that God will somehow recognize and bless this apparently good work. But it doesn't make them better than other people. They will still be sinners, they will still be saved by grace.

And above all we must remember not to make a show of our fasting. That warning came from Jesus. He saw and He knew how hypocritical were these fasts of the Pharisees. They didn't fast to improve themselves but only to be seen of men. They were not sad because their fasting reminded them of their great spiritual need, but they disfigured their faces to be seen of men. Do not make an exhibition of your fasting.

During Lent we discipline the body that the soul may prosper. Physically, materially, and spiritually a Lenten fast should abundantly bless. We do well always to remember how the Pharisees failed in their fast. They paraded their practice, their lips spoke one thing but their lives were not in harmony.

We are not to give up something that is wrong, for if it is wrong, it is so at any time. It ought never be practiced by the Christian. Fasting is really giving up non-essentials that we may gain a better hold of essentials. It is merely exchanging temporal things for eternal values. If Lent prompts us to fight out some besetting sin or evil habit we should by the grace of God be rid of it for all time.

In our fasting as in all else let us be prompted by the highest motives. We enter the fast for Christ's sake. Having attained Him we shall learn much and more.

Then when we have fasted and emptied our lives of a few things which we probably will miss, it is good to remember that there is never a vacuum in the heart. It will soon be filled again with many things. Let us by the grace of God fill it with things that are good. The amount of good that you supply—or—better said—you let God supply, will be a test of your earnestness. If you think more of your own convenience, your work, your likes and your dislikes, your preferences and your pleasures than you do of God's will, you are not taking these things very seriously. Will you let a few of your ordinary engagements go for the sake of your soul? No, they are not wrong or sinful, but you need more time for your soul.

Attend your Lenten services. It is a special season and you must approach it in a special way. These services are designed to help us in that approach. There is a feast of public worship during Lent. Sermons are especially prepared to show and to create need, awaken soul hunger. Attention is directed to God's special way of satisfying that need. Christ will come to you. You will recount the closing days of our Lord's ministry that you may better understand the awful consequences of your sin and the sacrifice that Jesus made for you. You will see visions as vast as God's love when you go to the upper room, or over Kidron, or you see the betrayal, the mock trial, or you stand before

Calvary and the cross. Doesn't it bring you closer to God? It's good to have others worshipping with us too. To know that we all have the same need and the same Savior. Do not miss your Lenten services.

Strange, isn't it, how great our hunger is and yet we devote so little time to reading the Word of God which is called the "bread of life." Ought we not give more time to careful reading and meditation? Much has been done to make the Bible and an abundance of devotional literature available. Take time to read and nourish your soul. The Bible meets all your vital needs whatever your circumstances may be. Have you really made a serious attempt at finding there, something that would satisfy a persistent need? You may not find it at once. Repeated readings, especially of the Gospels, may be required.

> Give me the old family Bible,
> Let me feel of its thumbed pages and its dirty edges,
> Let me take it upon my knees and read
> From its familiar pages by the dim light of day,
> As did my fathers before me.
> Give it to me now as the light fast fades out of the sky,
> Give me the old family Bible.

Many are the hearts that have been led by its sacred pages to find peace, contentment, happiness, and joy. Maybe Lent was made especially for you this year. Read the story about Jesus again—won't you?

Then let your heart speak with God in prayer. Blessed privilege it is to engage in thoughtful, earnest, unselfish prayer. To search our hearts and to pour them out before a suffering and crucified Savior. He will speak to you, too. Only those who try will ever know the peace and joy that prayer brings. Sometimes it is the Lord's Prayer—and that is the "perfect prayer"—sometimes it will be a treasured prayer from childhood—and then again a few words stammered forth by a faith that is frail. But God listens and He hears. Just a sigh, just a word, and the flood-gates of God's immeasurable sea of mercy are opened and showers of blessings are poured out upon you.

Helping others may also help us. God's kingdom is builded through agencies that are human. Put in a few extra hours for others during Lent. Christ will reach other lives through yours. What a harvest there would be if all would lend a hand. Are you working and sharing? Deny yourselves a few luxuries that you may have more to share with others. That's good Lenten discipline.

Lent! Yes. Let us keep the feast sincerely and trust our future to Christ.

Chapter 12

Sorrows – Ill and Good

Great is my boldness of speech toward you, great is my glorying of you: I am filled with comfort, I am exceeding joyful in all our tribulation.

For, when we were come into Macedonia, our flesh had no rest, but we were troubled on every side; without were fightings, within were fears.

Nevertheless God, that comforteth those that are cast down, comforted us by the coming of Titus;

And not by his coming only, but by the consolation wherewith he was comforted in you, when he told us your earnest desire, your mourning, your fervent mind toward me; so that I rejoiced the more.

For though I made you sorry with a letter, I do not repent, though I did repent: for I perceive that the same epistle hath made you sorry, though it were but for a season.

Now I rejoice, not that ye were made sorry, but that ye sorrowed to repentance: for ye were made sorry after a godly manner, that ye might receive damage by us in nothing.

For godly sorrow worketh repentance to salvation not to be repented of: but the sorrow of the world worketh death.

II Corinthians 7:4-10

SORROWS there are among all. Days of cloud and sunshine come and go. Days when we gathered roses and everything we touched turned to flowers and then again days when nothing but thorns remained. Days when we sang joyfully and then again days when music had no charms. Yes, sorrows there have been and always will be so long as we live in a sinful world. The first cause of all sorrow is sin, but its nature and its present and ultimate effect is as widely different as day and night.

Let us look for a moment at the two kinds of sorrow which the apostle here mentions: godly sorrow and the sorrow of the world.

The world has its sorrow. Let that be clear. Some may have gone the way of the world to escape the hardships and the sorrows of the Christian, but their hope to escape sorrow and trial was indeed vain. Do not be deceived into believing that the gaiety of the world is as real as it seems. Oftentimes a worldly good cheer is imposed upon a broken heart to cover a multitude of experiences never revealed. The hand of universal experiences touches everyone.

Especially does the world sorrow in times of disappointment. When the fondest hope crumbles and the most cherished plan is thwarted, then the worldly heart weeps without recourse. There are disappointments enough in the average life to kill a man who does not turn to God. How miserably small and helpless man is when left to himself.

Then there are bereavements and losses that have caused the world to shed many tears. They have cried into the night and into darkness that was impenetrable and only the echoes of their own voices returned to them. But these were empty and void.—And there are vexing and annoying circumstances which surrounded them—always, it seems. Why must this be so and that continue thus? Discomfort, displeasure, and dissatisfaction stalk them everywhere. The world knows the strange despairing sorrow of sin too. Surely the world has sinned enough to have a broken heart. And broken it will be.

These are all sorrows which harbor death. Any one of them protracted long enough is sufficient to work death. And what a wreckage these despairing sorrows have wrought. "The wages of sin is death." When sorrows come the world knows not where to turn. There is no consolation and comfort; for no one but God can give these. There is no one to assist them in bearing the burden and surely no one to remove the burden. Only God can do that. And the world knows Him not. Not uncommon to hear that disappointment and the resultant despair has caused a suicide. Oh, how energetically and fearfully sorrow works in the hearts of those who have no hope.

Sin in all its forms causes sorrow to the unregenerate world. "Be sure your sin will find you out." But the world sorrows in its own way and without a merciful God to whom it may turn. A soul has transgressed and as a result is disgraced and avoided. Does he think about the experience as sin? Yes, but only in the light of present consequences. He fears the sin only because of his personal loss in his social and business relationships. His grief is selfish and his heart remains the same. Only God can change that.

A man is untrue to the one he has sworn to cherish and to love. His sin is discovered and he finds himself stranded without home and friends. Sorrow—indescribable. But he would sin again if it could be done without detection.

A man entrusted with a responsible office is unfaithful in the discharge of his duties, or he embezzles the funds entrusted to his care and is convicted by law and sent to a penal institution. He may have remorse and regret because of the exposure and the immediate consequences but he does not therefore necessarily hate sin or regret his mistake for sin's sake. He may be brought to repentance but then the motive of his sorrow will change. The thought of those he has injured and shamed by his sin may add to his grief, but in the whole matter all these things are of secondary concern. He would sin again if he could do it without being found out.

The sorrow of the world which has only the immediate consequences in mind is surely a sorrow that worketh death. It produces distress without relief. It breaks the heart finally and lacerates the hardest spirit, destroying the peace and marring forever the life of such a one. The heart remains the same for only God can change that, and His aid is not invoked.

When God pronounced His judgment upon Cain, the passionate resentment of the first murderer found expression in a selfish utterance, "My sin is greater than I can bear." Such too was the selfish sorrow of King Saul when Samuel told him that because of his disobedience the kingdom would be taken from him, "I have sinned, yet honor me now before the elders of the people." Yes, and with Judas, the consciousness of sin, when he saw the awful consequences, plunged him into hopeless remorse and abandoned despair. "He went out and hanged himself." That's the way of the world. Its sorrow always works death. It is true that if we cannot turn to God and see our sorrow and sin in the light of His forgiving countenance, the issue will be death. Always it becomes darker. One excess leads to another. The world gets what it wants and then suffers for it.

But here the apostle speaks about another sorrow which he calls godly sorrow. God sees sin not in the light of the consequences but in the light of Himself. He sees sin as rebellion against Him, a thing infinitely wicked in itself. Sorrow for sin according to God is to see it as He sees it. If there were no God there would be no sin. Therefore the first element in godly sorrow is a sense that I have displeased and grieved my Father in heaven and my Savior. It is not the thought of the penalty that oppresses here. It is not the Father's frown which frightens us, but His grief. And that sorrow melts and subdues the heart to a real contrition and the thought is, How could I have grieved my God and Father thus? Your cry to Him in such a need is both a wish and a hope to be delivered from the power and the pollution of any sin.

Law and the fear of hell may startle into sorrow, but it is the great power of Christ's love which melts the heart into true repentance. "You may hammer ice to pieces but it is ice still." Dread of punishment may grind the soul in distress but it does not change the heart. But sorrow after God worketh a true repentance. Repentance is a comprehensive word. It is more than penitence, more than a regretful sense. It is this and more for it includes the refuge and the shelter that we seek in Christ. Feeling may not always be a great element, though it may also almost overwhelm us. We recognize this in repentance, that one who has lived in sin finally seeks his refuge in the shelter God has provided.

That type of sorrow brings no regrets. The discovery of sin and its vileness may be bitter but there is not one step in true repentance that we would miss. Though we sow in tears we reap in joy. "Weeping may endure for a night, but joy cometh in the morning." How such sorrow softens and relieves the heart. We had done something wrong at home—we often did. Our hearts ached and we struggled long to tell and then finally amid incoherent sobs we told our little story to mother and we came into a new world. Darkness was dispersed and the sun of parental grace shone once more. So it is with a sin sick soul falling upon the Savior's breast. Unutterable sorrow is transformed to unspeakable joy. If you have had that experience you will know why you treasure your relationship with Jesus.

Consider the prodigal son in the parable. Was it the shame, was it the bad name he had acquired by his riotous living, was it the fortune he had wasted that made him sorrow? No. As he stumbled that long way home to the father's house they heard him say out of a broken heart, "I have sinned against heaven and against thee." And Peter—it came upon him forcibly when he saw the Savior's face that he had sinned against Him. There lay the awfulness of his sin. "And Peter went out and wept bitterly." Blessed Peter.

Thanks be to God for His gracious goodness.

Chapter 13

Renunciation and Faith

*But what things were gain to me, those I counted loss
for Christ.*

*Yea doubtless, and I count all things but loss for the
excellency of the knowledge of Christ Jesus my Lord: for
whom I have suffered the loss of all things, and do count
them but dung, that I may win Christ,*

*And be found in him, not having mine own righteous-
ness, which is of the law, but that which is through the
faith of Christ, the righteousness which is of God by
faith.*

Philippians 3:7-9

STRANGE paradox is this. Paul speaks of losses
that were gains and of gains that were losses.
We can understand the estimates better when we
know that life must be considered from two sides
—both the internal and the external. We must
reckon alike the visible and the invisible values,
the spiritual and the physical. To properly evalu-

ate life one must observe it with the eyes of Scripture. Here the spiritual is always stressed and the physical is invariably secondary.

One might feel that the words of our text were the hasty words of youth where judgments sometimes are impassioned, lacking in deliberate and careful analysis. The fact is, the words were spoken by Paul when he was a well matured Christian who had gathered about him the wisdom of experience. Paul the aged was uttering words of knowledge accumulated through the joyful and sorrowful vicissitudes of a veteran's life. A man who had been worshipped and then stoned, a man who had been imprisoned at Philippi and who had been at home in cultured Athens, a man who knew every bay in the Adriatic and who silver-haired had stood before Nero in Rome's court of justice, has spoken—uttered his convictions. His testimony must be worth listening to. He is preeminently qualified to speak.

Let us look at a few of the things which Saul of Tarsus renounced when he became Paul the apostle. He turned his back upon inherited privileges. And these were many. He was circumcised on the eighth day—he was a Jew. He was a descendant of the founder of the race, of the tribe of Benjamin, the most distinguished of all the tribes. All in all it could be said of him that he was a Hebrew of the Hebrews. He shared the inner circle. He had taken no little pride in this inherited pre-eminence, but it didn't mean a thing to him any more.

He had taken his religion seriously, for he attached himself to the Pharisees, a church party which was most scrupulous in its observance of the ritualistic orders. So zealous had he been that he persecuted the church. So loyal had he been to Judaism, its traditions and its tenets, that he sought to destroy Christianity. Saul was motivated by deep convictions and a real concern. There was not much else that Saul could have done to rate high as a Hebrew and as a Pharisee. He had a high place in the inner circle and the record he had established was enviable. Pharisaism would expect great things from a young man so promising.

When he had met Jesus on the way to Damascus that day when the authorization papers from the chief priests shrivelled up in his bosom, he renounced all these privileges and the place of pre-eminence assigned to him by popular acclamation. And yet he is very reverent as he refers to the past, and he speaks of the faith of his fathers with respect. He didn't forget that through long years Judaism had been his only divine spiritual teacher and only interpreter. There was an ancient and hallowed glow that surrounded the economy which he abandoned. But it was after all an economy which had outlived its usefulness — its mission had already been accomplished. He was not slow to recognize that there was glory in that which was to be put aside but he was equally bold in affirming its worthlessness in comparison with the greater glory of that which now had been revealed to him. Paul knew that the most precious things have no value when compared to Christ. Before he attained his knowledge of Christ he had deemed the things he now gladly renounced, as the most precious of all. "It would be positive loss if a man were to shut up his windows and go to work by candlelight when the sun was shining brightly."

If men continue in that which is lesser and imperfect when God has revealed the excellency of Christ, it will be to them a great loss. "It is a loss if we persist in creeping and crawling along amid the things of earth when Christ has sent His Spirit to bear our hearts and souls to heaven." He was a bad Jew, an apostate Pharisee discredited by his own people—but he did have Christ. Then nothing mattered much. Oh, for a clearer vision of Christ.

Now what had Paul really gained? He gained Christ and all that this implies. Now Paul would not have us believe that because he had renounced so much he also had merited much in return. That would of course have been inconsistent with the character of Paul and the nature of the new economy of faith. The renunciation, the giving up, the counting of all things as loss, followed but did not precede the gift. When he received the gift of salvation in Christ he began to lose interest in all other things and he let go of them.

Among Paul's gains was "the excellency of the knowledge of Christ Jesus." As a knowing and as a thinking man Christ appealed to him. Christ was a reality. The righteousness of Christ was to him no dream or idle speculation. Here he stood face to face with fundamental reality. His knowledge of Christ's merits demanded his appreciation and a complete surrender. He had come under the spell of Christ's transforming influence. And Saul of Tarsus was recreated, transformed into the likeness of his Savior. His whole being was transformed.

Within the heart of Paul a new loyalty was created which found expression in love and obedience. Paul calls Christ "my Lord." Christ became the ruler of his life and the more he knew about Him, the more absolutely did he yield Him obedience in all things. "I was obedient to the heavenly vision." Not until we obey Christ, can we know how easy is His yoke and how beautiful and noble are His commandments.

Paul proved his creed by his deeds. He continued to do just that against the most violent opposition and persecution. "He suffered the loss of all things"—all things were taken from him. These were the damages assessed against him when he became a follower of Christ. And he endured. He endured, "that I might be found in him," that is, found in the righteousness of Christ. There was a time when he thought he would and could stand before God in his own merits, but now all had changed. After he had seen Christ he abandoned that idea. Frankly he was ashamed. He couldn't come before God and say: I am a Hebrew, I am a Pharisee, here is my righteousness, acquired through painstaking effort as a Pharisee. No righteousness except in Christ. And Paul, whatever the cost, took his shelter in this sure refuge.

Man must be right with God. Paul took that for granted. By one means or another, God and man must be brought together. There must be reconciliation and peace. We can arrive at terms of peace not by presenting anything we have done, but only through the medium of Christ's righteousness. We could not fulfill the law, He fulfilled it for us. Only one perfect life has ever been lived. That life was the life of Jesus, Son of God and Son of man. Our faith in Him receives the merit of His life.

What of the past in which we have gathered guilt and doom? He died as He lived, all in our stead. Thus on the cross He bore our curse and

44291

cleared us from every judgment and opened wide the gates of God's kingdom.

The vicarious atonement has been assailed and assaulted, but still it stands and like a Rock of Ages it shall endure. How could He suffer and die for men? And yet the awakened conscience to the end of time will gravitate to the vicarious atonement as the one and only satisfying rest. There is a mystery there which we cannot understand or explain, but we can by the grace of God believe it.

Paul's later experiences approved the exchange that he had made. He has had ample time to review his life when this letter was written to friends at Philippi. He had tested his choice. Life had been viewed by him under many aspects. He had labored among the rude and the intelligent, among the impoverished and the wealthy. There was the hatred of his countrymen which he had to face, persecutions by Jews and Gentiles alike, the perils of travel, the exhaustion of manual labor. Yet now when life has been thoroughly tested by him he reiterates his choice. In Nero's prison cell at Rome, and within what seemed the shadow of death, Paul ratifies the choice that he had made thirty years before. I have never heard of anyone who on his death bed regretted choosing Christ whatever the cost involved.

How truly Jesus spoke when He said, "Whosoever would save his life shall lose it; and whoso-

ever shall lose his life for my sake shall find it."
Life properly begins with renunciation. By giving
up that which the world calls life, Paul acquired
that which was far superior. It was a life with an
outlook blessed with hope in death.

We do need resignation. "He that has once thoroughly yielded to God will eventually yield to
nothing but God."

Chapter 14

Why Are We Here?

I pray not that thou shouldest take them out of the world, but that thou shouldest keep them from the evil.
They are not of the world even as I am not of the world.
Sanctify them through thy truth: thy word is truth.
John 17:15-17

> *In an age on ages telling,*
> *To be living is sublime.*

L IFE is complicated, intense, but rich in possibilities, and fraught with many dangers. It is interesting and livable. Strange, isn't it? For many people it is hard to live, but it is harder still to leave. Life seems to be a constant adversity, yet when the call to depart comes they would rather stay. Life has a peculiar quirk, but it can be beautiful.

Jesus is much concerned about His disciples. He knew them so well. They had been so slow of heart to believe; they learned with difficulty. They had been impatient and selfish; they had made many mistakes in judgment.

Aware how difficult the assignments would be for them, how bitter and subtle the world would be, knowing the sufferings they would be called upon to endure, Jesus spent the closing hours of His life interceding for them. He prayed for them with words so fervent they must have burned themselves upon their hearts. He knew how God could transform these fishermen into servants of heroic valor. The world would be enraptured by the story of their spiritual exploits. He saw the thousands that would stand triumphant amid the flames that devoured them. God's love would make them anew, transform them and steel them with endurance that would be the marvel of the ages.

But He did know how hard put they would be to remain faithful so He prays, "I pray not that thou shouldest take them out of this world, but that thou shouldest keep them from the evil one." He did not ask for them the security of some secluded nook where they would be untouched by the transient pleasures and sorrows of this world, where they would be unharmed and untouched by the politics, the business, and the labor of this world. He prayed that in the midst of these they might be kept—preserved from evil.

After all, the world was to be their sphere of activity. That was to be the scene of their witnessing and their labor. However keenly they might wish to escape the taunts and the threats of a wicked world, it was necessary for themselves, for the world, and for their Master's sake, that they stay as the salt and leaven of the human family. As they walk in the midst of life, Satan's finger must not defile them. Shadrach, Meshach, Abednego, and Daniel in the court of Darius are typical Old Testament examples of what can be done, what a life can be lived in the midst of an evil and perverted environment. All of the disciples of Jesus were preserved in the faith save Judas who perished, a victim of his own lust for money.

Could we escape all evil by returning into solitude? No. One could escape the world in that way but self and Satan would still remain to harass. These are inescapable and, in fact, are often most dangerous in solitude or retirement. We conclude that there are many dangers on every side and that the world is a hard place.

But we are here because God has put us here. We are placed here to be trained for a higher life. Time and a few trials seem necessary that the Spirit of God may restore in our hearts a more perfect image of God. A few years and a few trials and some flower into perfection while others may require long protracted trials through bitter years before they mature. But "the fitness of the character and the greatness of the work is often measured by the duration of the trial." "The fairest flower blooms in the blackest soil, and the tallest tree springs heavenward from the rocks." "Whereever lives are being tried in whatever common place and homely ways, there God is hewing out the pillars for His temple." Job uttered the same truth when he said, "When he has tried me I shall come forth as gold." The violet appears early and blossoms quickly and is gone too soon, but the oak has matured through centuries of storm and is become the shelter for a thousand herds. Times will be trying, when we say, "Oh, that I had in the wilderness a lodging place for wayfaring men." Or we may say with Job, "I long to be where the wicked cease from troubling and the weary are at rest." But remember please, that not an hour of time, not a single agony is lost. Every experience is translated into strength and usefulness.

We must remain in the world for the sake of others too. Man does not live to himself alone. Amid the cares and the temptations of this world we must pass a time of sojourn that God's purpose may be accomplished upon others. "As thou hast sent me into the world, even so have I also sent them into the world." God could have sent angels in spotless raiment white as snow, to preach the gospel, but He didn't wish to do the preaching that way. He might have sent angels to visit the fatherless and widows, but He didn't. It was work to be done in another way. He might have sent angels to minister food and raiment to the poor, to bring comfort and help to the unfortunate, but He didn't. Surely He might have sent emissaries from His holy place to live so well that evil-doers would be ashamed—but He didn't. No, these honorable functions He entrusts to men and women —His people. Then it is easy enough to understand why Christ does not want His disciples to withdraw from the world. The throng and the turmoil have a claim upon them. "Behold the fields white unto the harvest." There is much to do and the time is short.

Does the evil against which Christ prays here, consist of the outward tribulations, trials, and troubles of life in poverty, bereavements, and bodily suffering? Christ knew that "man is born unto trouble as the sparks fly upward," but He obviously referred to a greater evil. The evil to which He refers and which filled His heart with apprehension was more deadly and would by all means, fair or foul, seek to separate us from the love of God and His fellowship. That is the peril we must learn to recognize. Our environment is filled with vicious influences steadily at work seeking to destroy our faith, and with it our souls as well. Never make light of these dangers however slight they may seem to be. The prayer of Jesus is a cry of warning to us lest we pause to listen to the siren song of unbelief. The craft and cunning of the tempter is seductive and the lures that he extends may be too much for us. St. Paul does not under-rate our peril. It is real. "Our wrestling is not against flesh and blood, but against hosts of wickedness in heavenly places." That's Paul's warning to us and to all Christians of all time. This business of living in a world of wickedness is serious. The god of this world, the powers of this world, the men of this world, and the things of this world are all in their degree fighting against the man who believes. By the grace of God it will take all your astuteness and all your energies to enable you to survive. And the same rule applies to all. Except for the grace of God you would be vanquished before the day is done. You cannot move in any direction but the devil instantly sets out some creature to attack you. But there is one whom the devil fears and that is Christ who with a word can force him to desist and be gone. There is no other way. Let us make sure that Jesus is at our side and we "need fear no ill, with Him at hand to bless."

It is possible to live in this world with its manifold evil complexes and still remain unspotted, like a flower floating in the grimy waters of some bog. Botanists tell of a so-called enamel plant which radiates purity though it grows in coal mines amid the dust and the grime there. Nothing can stain its snowy enamel whiteness.

To further characterize the whiteness and the purity of the Christians would only add more to the utter humility we now feel. We say softly but very earnestly, "God be merciful to me a sinner." And there isn't much more we can say. Our heavenly Father will understand what we mean. But for the fact that we have been laid upon the heart of Israel's Keeper, we would despair. But for the sanctifying, cleansing power of the truth of God, we would be lost. But for the interceding love of Jesus Christ our Savior, we would never make it. For God, however, "nothing is impossible."

Chapter 15

The Greatest Wonder of All

But when the fulness of the time was come, God sent forth his Son, made of a woman, made under the law,

To redeem them that were under the law, that we might receive the adoption of sons.

Galatians 4:4-5

"GOD so loved the world that he gave his only begotten son that whosoever believeth in him should not perish but have everlasting life." A strange love was that. That unworthy men who were sinful and wicked should so touch and move the heart of God is beyond our understanding. God really cared for all men and the extremity to which He went in demonstrating that love proves, beyond any question of doubt, the goodness of our Maker. God must have loved the world since He Himself came to redeem it by becoming one of us.

It is not so strange that this fact should startle Jews and Gentiles. For who had ever heard of such a God? It was new to them. Now some were startled to love and adoration and others were startled to hate and mockery and unbelief. Some when they heard the gospel of love became repentant, but many, in fact, most of them, only hated. The coming of God in the flesh will always be a stumbling block for many, but for those who repent and believe it will be the source of transcendent joy.

When did God reveal this Savior? The Word tells us. "When the fulness of time had come, God sent forth his son." God's plan is always good and He has a plan for every occasion.

All great movements within the kingdom have been planned and designed by God. He prepared the man and set the time. Maybe the man was taken out of obscurity where no one could claim the credit for training him. God sent him to begin the work at a season not too auspicious as viewed by the world, but the long range vision of the divine eye knew that the time was at hand. The man may have been found in the world of business or he may have been taken out of a desert wilderness. He may be rich or he may be poor. His usefulness depends upon his readiness to be guided by the voice of God. Such men are available and God knows where to find them. They shoulder re-

sponsibilities and they assume leadership so that
the plans of the kingdom shall not be frustrated.
Men may idolize them or they may hate them and
despise them. The world may not understand. The
servant of God, called upon to present a cause, or
usher in a new era, may be persecuted and even
put to death and yet God's plans shall not miscarry.

The greatest man who ever came to share the
burdens of mankind and to direct their destinies
was Jesus of Nazareth. Greatest because He was the
God-man, God incarnate. The world was in a bad
way, for "darkness covered the earth, and gross
darkness the peoples," and only a great spirit, the
Son of God, was equal to the situation. And He
came in the "fulness of time." Sooner would have
been too early, later would have been too late. He
came just when He was needed most and God's
economy of salvation found a full expression in
His life and in His death. Had He come at Isaiah's
time no one would have understood Him. Had He
come a century later there would have been no
opening for His kingdom. "He came to his own
and his own received him not," but a few disciples
who represented Hebrew life and thought did accept Him. Thus was given the humble fishermen
from Galilee the privilege of becoming the nucleus
in a kingdom destined to revolutionize the world.
Not strange that the preparatory period continued

so long, for the work to be accomplished was great. The wise old sage says, "To every thing there is a season, and a time for every purpose."

The historical preparation of the world for Christ is clear. Paul knew and understood the processes that had been completed. He was of Jewish birth and he knew the story of his race. He was a Roman citizen and all around him he could see the supremacy of this nation. He knew the intellectual strivings and the moral deterioration that marked the pre-Christian era. The kingdom now to be established was to be builded at the "confluence of three great civilizations"—the Jewish, Roman, and Greek. All these nations helped to complete what we know as the "fulness of time."

The main contribution of the Hebrew culture was to be found in their monotheistic religion. Idolatry was gone but legalism and ceremonialism had their ardent votaries. The people crying for bread were fed stones. Devoted hearts were tired and weary of the pharisaic mechanism and the hair-splitting controversies of their schools. People then as now wanted more of God and less of sophistry. The popular expectation of a Deliverer was quite pronounced.

The Greeks made their contribution to the "fulness of time" too. That was intellectual. "God moves in a mysterious way His wonders to perform." The Greeks were to be the vehicle of diffusion. Here too, the people were dissatisfied with the old religious faiths which were rapidly crumbling. Pitiless criticism of Greek philosophy was a contributing factor. But while philosophy could criticize it could not satisfy the higher aspirations. But out of Greece came the language for the most beautiful and the most satisfying story ever told.

The rapidly expanding Roman empire facilitated the spread of that story. Her rising power and the peace that prevailed created a specially favorable time for the diffusion of Christianity. Peace always assures freedom of communication and the Roman roads facilitated rapid transit to every corner of the empire. The time was auspicious for a missionary campaign.

If Christ had come a hundred years earlier Rome would have had no authority in Judea. Rome would have had no part in His persecution, and the crucifixion could not have been perpetrated as foretold. Had the Messiah come a hundred years later, the Jewish people would have been destroyed, the temple in ruins and the people in exile. He came when the religious, intellectual, and political conditions were so prepared. He came in the "fulness of time."

When He did come the world was all at peace but darkness prevailed. It was no accident that He came then. His coming closes an old epoch and opens a new one. "The time receptacle into which the centuries and the millenniums had been poured was full up to the precise moment when this great event should be added; and it was added just then."

He was "born of a woman, born under the law." His birth was not His beginning. He was sent and His origin lies in eternity. He comes and He assumes the form of a man but He belongs to the ages. He took upon Himself the cares and experiences of humanity—He shared our emotions, wept our tears. He hoped and He feared, was subject to changes and in everything but sin was a man among men. He came as a native, not in angelic array. He was a descendant of David and He bore the marks of Nazareth—one of the common people. There is the mystery of the incarnation.

It was necessary for Him to observe the law as common men observed it. The Son must be obedient, even to death upon the cross. All His life He was under the law. Nor did He ever transgress it. No flaw nor fault could be found by those who sought to destroy Him.

Perhaps the most startling thing about His labors was the limitations of His divine power, the degree to which He emptied Himself of power. Yes, God was there but the splendor of Jehovah was veiled under the mechanism of a flesh that was frail; and yet there throbbed beneath a lowly exterior the energy which created the universe.

God manifests Himself in many ways through history, nature, and conscience, but here we have a supremely personal and unique revelation of Himself.

And when He thus came it was for this purpose, "That he might redeem them that were under the law, that we might receive the adoption as sons." Here we find in these few words the sum and substance of the entire Gospel. He came to buy back that which was held by another. Where there was no way He made one. We were in abject slavery and we could do nothing about it. Then who should deliver us? God alone could do that and He paid the ransom. What price did He pay? "Not with gold nor silver but with His holy, precious blood and innocent sufferings and death." Why did He pay such a price? "That I might be His own," belong to Him. Then if I belong to Him I am no longer a lost and condemned creature. We are His property, purchased to be His children by adoption and we shall serve Him gladly and faithfully. I am ready.

Chapter 16

Something Is Wrong

Ye ask, and receive not, because ye ask amiss, that ye may consume it upon your lusts.

James 4:3

THE season of Lent should be prayerful. Prayer is intended for all time and all occasions, but it seems especially fitting during a time when by the grace of God we are seeking to build up our faith. God knows all the difficulties we face and how weak and ineffective our faith seems to be. Who can stand before the cross repeatedly as we do during this season without a sense of deep guilt arising in our hearts? And that sense of guilt virtually compels us to seek our refuge in Christ and in His redemption. He volunteered to make a way for us, to make a way where there was no way and where all human endeavors had failed and would fail. Surely God's concern for us was real or the

Good Friday scenes would never have been enacted. God would not have permitted hell to vent its wrath on the Son of man no matter how dramatic the story might have been, unless the epic unfolded there effectively expressed His love and our need.

That is what we want to understand better—the meaning of the cross. The cross makes a lot of difference. Surely it meant much to God—can it mean less to us?

Nothing will reveal the glory of the cross to us but a careful, Spirit-filled searching of the Word of God and a constant, prayerful calling upon the name of God. "Lord, teach us to pray."

Blessed is the man who has cultivated the prayer spirit and who can hold communion with God and release the vast resources of His power. That's why the Word of God exhorts to prayer without ceasing. Great men of God have also been men of prayer. But not until the cross energized prayer were the floodwaters of God's mercy really opened.

It would be needless to ask, Do you pray? Or do you maybe think that you can manage without it? Can you face your daily task, can you bear the burdens, endure the sorrows incident to life without looking unto God?

But you say prayer hasn't seemed to help. I have prayed about my task; when sorrows came I have taken them to God and when the burdens were many I brought them to Him. I never felt that they were answered. Then we would conclude that there was something wrong. Not anything wrong with prayer, but something is wrong with the way you pray. James in his Epistle says, "Ye have not because ye ask not," and he adds, "Ye ask and receive not because ye ask amiss."

To ask amiss is to ask improperly or erroneously. Maybe that's your trouble. There may be something wrong with the motive. Maybe only dire necessity forces you to unburden yourself before God—it may be an expression of your selfishness. Such a prayer could not be expected to reach very far—certainly not to the throne of God.

We have been taught that to pray is to speak with God. That's how simple prayer is. But the Spirit which moves us to speak with God about anything, much or little, must be genuine and without guile or selfishness.

We might simplify the definition of prayer further by saying, to pray is to express oneself before God. It's an attitude, a relationship. Sometimes other expressions convey more than the words we speak. You sometimes speak of men who talk with their hands and faces. The hands and face reveal more than words can. Whatever the manner of expression, God knows the prompting influence.

Those of you who have children have learned

many things, and one of them is just this. You can see clear through them. One day your child came hurrying home. You knew as you saw the child that something unusual had happened. And as the child came nearer there was no need even to tell you that something had happened to make your child glad. Joy radiates. That same child returned another day, faltering, with steps that seemed too heavy. You knew at once that the child had been disappointed. There is no need to say anything. Probably it was a bad report card. But you knew. The face tells the story. Another day the child came running, with tear-filled eyes and you knew the child had been hurt. Not so much— and you knew that too—but tears flow so freely. But in joy, in disappointment and sorrow and pain you were their comfort. Just to be with you was enough. Not a word was said. After a bit maybe you said, "Now tell me all about it." You like to hear about these little comedies and tragedies. And some of your choicest memories are gathered out of these little experiences. He never said a word, but you knew.

Now God is our Father and we are His children. When we approach Him He knows our need. We may not be able to formulate our prayer into words but He knows anyway. Sometimes we have tried to pray and found we were incapable of any expression save the words of some childhood prayer. While we were yet afar off God saw our need and the petition was never uttered. Don't you suppose that was what happened to the prodigal and to Nicodemus? God grants us what we desire and more. Just as the child seeks its refuge in you, so the children of God seek their refuge in Him. It is good to be with Him though the heart be too full for words. But there can be no sham: prayers that are phoney avail nothing.

Here James speaks of prayers that are selfish. These are prayers amiss. Only the humble, unselfish spirit can stand before God. Only that spirit can really face God. And then it very often is not courageous. You are quick to recognize the motives in your child which prompt prayers. You have said, "Look at me." Would God see less than we do?

The prayer of the world is always selfish. And may it be said here that the prayers of some Christians are selfish too. They pray for everything that concerns them; but Jesus said, "Our Father." We can pray so very earnestly that God will bless something we are doing. Can we pray as earnestly and as diligently for someone else who is doing something just as important? Are we jealous? Maybe we feel as if the world belonged to us and that we for the task at hand had a claim upon all its resources. The greedy, proud and selfish spirit sometimes prevails.

What do you suppose will be the first reaction upon one who really is a child of God when he discovers that he stands in the presence of God? His prayer will first be the publican's prayer, "God be merciful to me a sinner."

War is productive of many prayers—some good, some bad. Perhaps the spirit of selfishness creeps in even here. We feel instinctively that our efforts should be crowned with victory, that whatever we do is right and that whatever the enemy does is wrong. That is of course a selfish way of prayer: it is amiss. Ought we not rather pray that truth, whatever that be, should be vindicated and peace restored when God's purpose has been fulfilled?

Even praying for our own boys may be selfish. We love them and there doesn't seem to be anything we so much want as their safe return. Maybe what we really ought to be praying for is that truth shall prevail whatever the cost to us might be.

This is a time of many answered prayers. Can you remember, not so long since, when it would have been impossible to let your boy go? But he was taken and strangely enough you could bear it because God gave you strength. The younger lad will be taken. Can you bear it? Wait and see.